W9-BAX-422

Roller Coasters

For Samantha and Spencer

And in memory of my mother and dad

Roller Coasters: United States and Canada

second edition

by
TODD H. THROGMORTON

McFarland & Company, Inc., Publishers
Jefferson, North Carolina, and London

On the cover: Two Face: The Flip Side, roller coaster at Six Flags America in
Largo, Maryland.

Library of Congress Cataloguing Data

Throgmorton, Todd H., 1962–
Roller coasters : United States and Canada / by Todd H. Throgmorton.— 2nd ed.
p.   cm.
Includes index.
ISBN 0-7864-0896-0 (illustrated case : alkaline paper) ∞
1. Roller coasters — United States — Directories.   2. Roller coasters — Canada —
Directories.   3. Amusement parks — United States — Directories.   4. Amusement
parks — Canada — Directories.   5. Roller coasters — History.   I. Title.
GV1860.R64T47   2000   791'.06'873 — dc21   00-25508

British Library cataloguing data are available

Manufactured in the United States of America

McFarland & Company, Inc., Publishers
Box 611, Jefferson, North Carolina 28640
www.mcfarlandpub.com

Acknowledgments

I'd like to begin this second edition as I did the first: by thanking the amusement parks listed in the book for providing valuable historical information along with the photos of their roller coasters. Thanks also to the following design firms: Arrow Dynamics, Bolliger & Mabillard, Great Coasters International, D.H. Morgan Manufacturing, Premier Rides, Wieland Schwarzkopf, and Vekoma International. Their informative assistance offered a unique perspective on the creative process.

In tracking down historic photos, Paul Ruben, the Museum of the City of New York, the Denver Public Library, the Library of Congress, Judith Walsh of the Brooklyn Public Library, Ann Parker with the Santa Cruz Beach Boardwalk, and Susan Hormuth, an independent researcher, proved to be of tremendous help. To them I express my gratitude.

Thanks also to my brother Adam for the use of Global Architectural Models' photographs and to Terry Scott for his computer proficiency.

Finally, I want to thank my wife Susan for all her support and assistance on this project — which seems to be always expanding. In the seven years since the first edition the number of coasters in North America has more than doubled, and although the census is still far below the 1929 peak, this is good news for roller coaster connoisseurs everywhere.

Contents

History

Anticipation! Some call it fear; the feeling in the pit of your stomach as you slowly climb that long first hill, anxiously awaiting and imagining just what lurks beyond.

There is the slow creaking clickity-clack of the lift chain as it pulls you closer toward that first drop. As the train tops out, the passengers in the first few seats are dangled menacingly for a moment, allowing them one last look around at what will soon be a blur.

Then it happens. That sudden plunge as you fall like a rock, experiencing the "rush" that addicts you. From there the excitement of a series of dips and negative G-forces follows as you coast over the hills or through several highbanked fan curves that throw you from side to side.

This is a roller coaster!

The roller coaster is an American tradition, a part of our heritage, and in some cases, a link to the past. Maybe our parents or grandparents rode the same coasters that we ride today. The stories that can be told in recollection of those rides and the legends that are created are numerous. There may also be a celebrity connection to coasters such as aviation pioneer Orville Wright's fondness of the Coney Island Cyclone or the favorite of Elvis Presley, the Zippin Pippin in Memphis. However, in most cases, it is the roller coaster itself that has attained celebrity status.

The roots of the roller coaster can be traced back to Russia in the late sixteenth and early seventeenth century. A Russian sport of this time was known as ice sliding, a winter recreation that was popular for nearly 200 years. Ice slides were first constructed by a Russian entrepreneur who discovered a basic principle that has become a foundation upon which the appeal of the roller coaster was built: People will actually pay to be terrified.

The concept behind the Russian ice slides was simple. A 70-foot wooden tower provided the initial starting point from where a 2-foot long sled plunged down the ramp covered with ice. Each rider would sit on the lap of an experienced guide who steered the sled down the ramp and across a length of approximately 600 feet, coming to a stop at the base of another 70-foot tower. At this point the guide and his passenger would climb up the second tower to repeat the ride in the opposite direction, bringing them back to the original tower.

Due to their popularity, these ice slides could be found in cities and villages all over Russia, and the Russian royalty fancied the adventure. Ice slides near St. Petersburg were even strung with colored lanterns along the straightway to provide for night sliding.

Of course, the ice needed to create an ice slide made the ride strictly a win-

Vincent Price on the Giant Dipper for the 1978 television documentary "America Screams" (Bill Lovejoy).

Ice sliding in St. Petersburg in 1610 (Paul L. Ruben archives).

ter activity — until Catherine the Great had sleds fitted with tiny wheels so she could operate her ride during the warm months as well. This was the first of many refinements that would bring us the modern roller coaster.

In the late eighteenth century, a French traveler became fascinated with this unique Russian entertainment and took the idea home. The French adapted the ice slide to the milder Parisian climate by using a track made of closely spaced rollers, similar to a modern conveyer, on which sleds with runners could coast. This is the origin of the name roller coaster, a name which has endured even after the disappearance of coasting courses.

It was not long before the idea of replacing the sled runners with wheels took root. The first of these new recreational attractions made its debut at a public garden in the Ternes Quarter of Paris in 1804.

As the thrill became addictive, it inspired other French inventors to make improvements to the principal design. These new-fangled roller coasters appeared in picnic gardens throughout France much to the delight of the public. One such example was the Bellevue Mountains built in a Paris suburb during 1817. This coaster eliminated the need for climbing to a second tower for a return trip; instead, the sled simply gained enough speed down the first ramp to bring it up a second ramp, concluding at the top of the second tower where the ride repeated in reverse.

To take this idea one step further, a coaster named the Promenades Aeriennes made its debut as the first to allow

Russian Mountains in Paris, France, 1816 (Paul L. Ruben archives).

passengers a return trip to their original starting point without stopping. The tracks were built in a circular form, and at the bottom of the initial drop, the track was banked so that the cars kept enough momentum to propel them up the incline and back into the station.

The Promenades Aeriennes coaster was chock full of innovations. In terms of safety, it was the first coaster designed with guide rails to keep the cars from jumping the track — an important attribute considering that these cars rounded the corners at more than 40 miles per hour, which was a considerable speed in the early 1800s.

The Promenades Aeriennes was also the first racing coaster. Two identical tracks ran side by side down the first 80-foot drop; at the bottom they split off, going in opposite directions. After completing the circular track, they came together again at the station.

This era of French coaster history provided a solid foundation from which to build, but for some unknown reason

Cherrelyn Street Railway (Denver Public Library: Western History Department).

the French seemed to lose interest. The fad of the French "coasters" passed from fancy as quickly as it had arrived.

The French contributions to fundamental roller coaster design should have been used to build upon, but the development of the coaster in America backtracked and these innovations were ignored until "discovered" or "invented" by American designers. For example, in 1826 a Frenchman by the name of Lebonjer patented a lifting device that would pull, via cable, the loaded coaster cars up the first hill; in fact, this is where the terms "lift hill" and "first drop" originated. The American coasters, however, did not incorporate the lift hill for several years. Regardless, it was the Americans who truly developed the roller coaster to its fullest potential.

The history of roller coasters in America is rooted in the mountains of Pennsylvania. The year was 1870 and an abandoned mine train was converted to passenger use for sightseeing. The cars on the inclined railway were originally used to haul coal down to the village of Mauch Chunk from the top of Mount Pisgah in eastern Pennsylvania. With the help of horses, the train would be pulled to the top of the mountain to be loaded; with the horses then secured on board the train, it would make the return trip down a slight grade, which is said to have only dropped 60 feet to the mile.

The passenger version followed the same routine, with the people riding to the top and then enjoying the 6 miles per hour journey back. Named the Mauch Chunk Railway, people lined up by the hundreds for the privilege of riding, paying a nickel each. In fact, the ride proved so popular that the railroads even ran special trains to accommodate the attraction.

The success of the Mauch Chunk Railway led to the construction of "artificial coasting courses" similar to those in France. Like the French predecessors, the tracks were originally made of rollers, giving birth to the American name "roller coasters." As in France, wheels mounted on the cars soon replaced the rollers, but the name was firmly ensconced in American slang.

The first unique roller coaster to appear in America was the Gravity Pleasure Switchback Railway at Coney Island, which made its debut in 1884. Although similar in principle to its French ancestors, the new coaster was unique with its undulating track, earning the inventor, La Marcus Adna Thompson, the nickname "Father of Gravity." Thompson's ride included a series of gentle waves along a 600-foot long track. Passengers sat sidesaddle to ride the wheeled cars, which reached top speeds of 6 miles per hour before coming to the end of the line. As with their predecessors, attendants had to push the cars up a second hill for the return trip.

Stories vary concerning Thompson's background and his ulterior motives in building the Switchback. One story refers to him as a Sunday school teacher from Philadelphia who wanted to divert young people from the popular beer gardens at Coney Island; another story credits him as a wealthy seamless hosiery inventor who saw an excellent business opportunity. Whatever the reason, by charging a nickel per ride, Thompson recovered his entire investment of $1,600 in just three weeks — to the utter amazement of his friends! This success inspired others to improve upon his ideas, triggering a coaster construction boom. Thompson himself went on to build twenty-four more coasters in

Hold on to your hat! (Library of Congress).

America and twenty in Europe, all exactly like his first.

Later in 1884, Charles Alcoke of Hamilton, Ohio, solved the "switchback" problem when he designed an oval track that returned passengers to the starting point, similar to the French Promenades Aeriennes. The phrase "out-and-back" was coined to describe the route of this track type. Alcoke's attraction, called the Serpentine Railway, achieved a top speed of 15 miles per hour while gliding over a series of mild hills and valleys.

Passengers sat sideways on these pioneering coasters until 1885, when Phillip Hinckle turned the seats forward with his new ride, the Gravity Pleasure

Switchback Railway (Library of Congress).

Road. A native of San Francisco, Hinckle also introduced the idea of a steampowered chain lift. With the combination of these inventions and refinements, an outbreak of coaster fever spread like a disease.

These improvements also meant that the Switchback coaster was obsolete, so Thompson decided to combine new ideas with a few more of his own, creating the ultimate roller coaster of the era. The Oriental Scenic Railway, as it was called, opened in Atlantic City in 1886. On this ride, the loaded cars were automatically pulled to the top of the first incline before being set free to the force of gravity. It was patented as a "scenic railway," referring to the picturesque scenes of the Orient painted on the walls of lighted tunnels, which riders viewed halfway through the ride. Since that time, the United States Patent Office in Washington, D.C., refers to all roller coasters as scenic railway.

Once again, Thompson's idea proved so successful that he was swamped with order requests. As a result, the L.A. Thompson Scenic Railway Company was formed to develop scenic railways throughout America. At the same time, others took out patents on their versions of scenic railways. Building them taller, longer, and faster, each was designed for more thrills than the competition.

It was not long before someone decided it was time to flip upside down on a roller coaster. The French experimented with this idea in 1846 when the first looping coaster opened at the Frascati Gardens. More of a spectacle than a ride, the loop stood 30 feet high and had a long straight run that was needed in order to gain momentum to complete the loop. The strain was too much on the

Top: Safety racer (1908) L.A. Thompson Scenic Railway (Historical File Warren Littlefield, Santa Cruz Seaside Co.). *Bottom*: French Centrifugal Railway (1846) (Paul L. Ruben Archives).

passengers, however, so the coaster was deemed unfeasible.

A similar lesson was learned in 1900 when Lina Beecher took the first step in turning American coaster riders upside

down on his loop ride, called the Flip-Flap. Located at Coney Island, this ride took less than 10 seconds, as a small car carrying two passengers coasted down an incline, picking up enough speed to

The Flip-Flap (Library of Congress).

complete the loop. Entering into the 30-foot-high perfect loop, it is said that a person would feel the equivalent force of 12 G's. The ride stirred interest but gave riders neck pains as the cars went through the loop. Before it was dismantled, people would pay to just watch the ride operate.

Although these first attempts at a looping coaster were far from perfect, they did encourage another inventor to try his hand. In 1901, Edward Prescott hired engineer E.A. Green to help him redesign the looping coaster. To lower the G-forces developed during the ride, they created a loop that was an oval rather than a true circle. Loop-the-Loop, as it was called, opened in Atlantic City as an engineering victory. Although this ride was the focus of much attention, it did not become a financial success due to its low rider turnover rate of four riders every five minutes. Turning coasters upside down would have to wait until the introduction of steel tracks in the early 1970s.

The first true standard roller coaster to appear at amusement parks during the turn of the century was the Figure-Eight. As the name hinted, the ride followed a track that wove over and under itself.

Like the scenic railway, the Figure-Eight was considered a wild, exciting ride. One such coaster designed by Fred Ingersoll and located at Kennywood Park in Pennsylvania between 1901 and 1921 was described by a writer for the

Top: Loop-the-Loop (Library of Congress). *Bottom:* Figure-Eight at Nantasket Beach (Library of Congress).

Pittsburgh Bulletin: "You were hauled up an incline in a gaudy little car and then let loose, down, under, over, through, up and around and back to the starting place at such a speed and by so many turnings and doublings that you lost all sense of direction and all coherence of ideas."

The fad of the Figure-Eight was short-lived, however, due to new innovations. By the 1920s, most of the original Figure-Eight had either been torn down or expanded and developed into more action-packed rides.

In 1909, John Miller introduced America to the racing coaster — and the final significant piece of engineering in this era of coaster design. The racing coaster featured two cars run side by side down mirror-image courses; the first car to the bottom won the "race."

But it was engineering innovation created by Miller with the racing coaster that revolutionized the ride. Miller attached a third set of wheels to the car under the track. Until now, the train relied on one set of wheels on top of the track and another set on the inside to create the side friction. This third set ensured safety by preventing the coaster trains from jumping the track while gliding over hills. Miller's third-wheel design is still the standard to this day.

The 1920s was the dawn of the Golden Age of roller coasters. World War I had ended and the economy was booming, resulting in a carefree America. The Roaring Twenties was a time of daredevilish challenge, and the coasters built during this decade reflect this attitude. New designs flourished with tracks twisting and turning in and out of dark

Figure-Eight in Coffeyville, Kansas (Library of Congress).

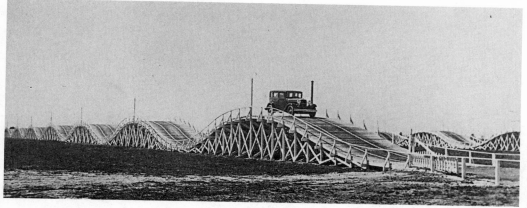

Top: Jack Rabbit Racer (1918) (Curt Teich Postcard Archives, Lake County, Illinois, Museum).
Bottom: Auto-coaster (National Archives).

tunnels and down first drops from a 100-foot-high lift. Names such as Cyclone, Blue Streak, Flying Turns, and Whirlwind were indicative of the new breed of coasters.

The number of coasters grew following the turn of the century to reach a peak of about 1,500 by 1929. Along with the growth of suburbs and an increasing number of automobiles, amusement parks appeared throughout the United States. Trolley lines were no longer the primary source of transportation, and parks became more accessible. In order to get people to drive to their park, each park owner would try

Top: Derby Racer in Vandalia, Illinois (Library of Congress). *Bottom:* Tornado/Bobs (1926–1977) (Library of Congress).

Cyclone (Brooklyn Public Library–Brooklyn Collection).

to build the highest, fastest and most terrifying coaster, beginning an era of roller coaster wars.

In 1927, the highest wooden coaster of the time was built in Poughkeepsie, New York: The Blue Streak was a 138-foot-high legend of the day. The Blue Streak battled the famous Cyclone, which is today the most popular remnant of the Golden Age.

Located at Coney Island's Astroland, the 1927 Cyclone is proof that quality survives. Even today it is the benchmark by which other coasters are judged. Designed by Vernon Keenan and Harry Baker, the Cyclone careens down an amazingly sharp 60-degree first drop, taking riders on an 85-foot plunge. Its earliest top speed has been lost to history, but today's Cyclone, with the help of bimetal rails and computers, averages 60 miles per hour. The trip along the rickety-sounding course takes just 1 minute and 40 seconds as passengers navigate its eight steep hills and valleys. As famed coaster designer John Allen said, "Part of the appeal is the imagined danger."

The Cyclone's imagined danger — along with the fact that the Cyclone paid off its $175,000 cost within the first year of its use — inspired many a roller coaster designer and park owner. Among these was Harry Traver. Notorious for many wicked coasters in the 1920s (all of which are now extinct), the name Traver became synonymous with Cyclone.

The scariest of the Traver creations were the Cyclones at Crystal Beach Park in Ontario, Canada; at Palisades Park in New Jersey; and the Lightning at Revere Beach, Massachusetts. Although regarded as wooden coasters, they were ac-

Cyclone at Crystal Beach (Paul L. Ruben Archives).

Aeroplane (1932) (Paul L. Ruben Archives).

tually steel structures with a layered wood track. They were enjoyed not only due to their height — they were 96 feet tall — but for what they did to one's body. They were fast, breathtaking, and rough; the Cyclone in Crystal Beach had a registered nurse on duty at all times. Although it existed only from 1928 to 1947, this coaster is still considered the most vicious ride ever.

Also built in 1928 was the Aeroplane coaster at Playland Amusement Park in Rye Beach, New York. For this coaster, Traver teamed up with Frederick Church. The spiral track banked so steeply that riders were slammed against the sides of the cars. The cars themselves tilted so far over that it appeared they would crash. This coaster was torn down in 1957, but was considered the masterpiece of the Golden Age.

During this era, the roller coaster lived through many transformations. The Golden Age was capped with the opening of the Bobs at Manchester, England, in 1929. This coaster took riders on an adventure that reached a maximum speed of 61 miles per hour. While this was the fastest coaster of the time, the Cyclone at Crystal Beach ranked as "the most fearsome," and the Bobs at Chicago's Riverview Park and the Aeroplane at Rye Beach were considered "the most beautiful."

Like so many other businesses, the roller coaster fell victim to the national economic woes of the Great Depression. The furious building pace of the Twenties screeched to a sudden halt. Park attendance was down. Owners could not afford to maintain coasters or pay for insurance. Hundreds of coasters were

Mountain Speedway (1935) (Curt Teich Postcard Archives, Lake County, Illinois, Museum).

abandoned or torn down and few new ones were built during the next forty years. Furthermore, World War II brought with it wood and rubber rationing, leading to the decline of old suburban amusement parks. From a Golden Age peak of around 1,500 rides, the coaster population dwindled to less than 200 by 1960.

By the mid–1950s, a revival of the roller coasters and theme parks was taking place in the United States. Since the Golden Age in the Roaring Twenties, the times had changed on all fronts — politically, economically, and socially.

Television had been introduced and almost immediately captured America's leisure time. The aging amusement parks of the past were now in direct competition with this new form of entertainment. When Walt Disney decided to create a park, however, he used this new medium to his advantage by promoting his new theme park with a show called "Disneyland." This successful marketing ploy led to the opening of Disneyland Park in Anaheim, California, on July 17, 1955.

Not too far from Disneyland, America's first "theme" park was still in operation — and had been since 1940. Old West Ghost Town was created by Walter Knott near his berry stand and was the first park to orient itself completely around a particular theme. As the years went on, more theme sections were added and the park evolved into Knott's Berry Farm (home of Mrs. Knott's famous chicken dinners).

Knott's modest beginning was helped considerably by the overwhelming success of Disneyland Park. Disneyland was the first planned theme park, and its opening marked the birth of the

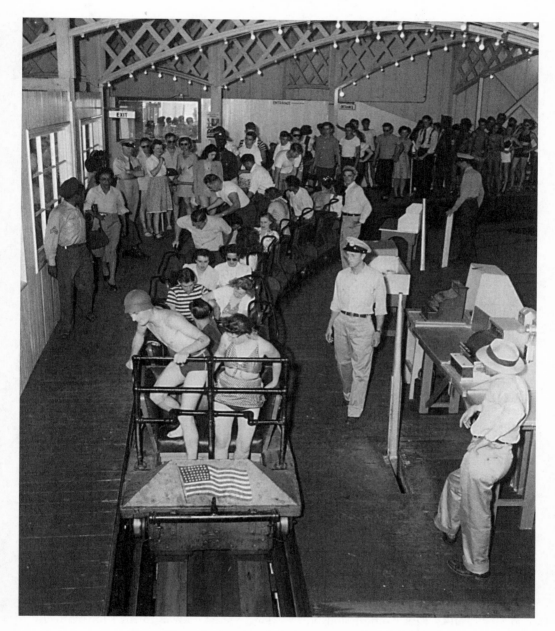

Giant Dipper Station (1946) (Santa Cruz Beach Boardwalk).

modern amusement park. As parks sprung up throughout the United States in the wake of Disneyland, it became apparent the revival of the roller coaster would soon follow.

The roots of the modern amusement park lie in the old amusement park with the only difference being that modern parks tend to revolve around a theme.

Traditional parks were first developed at Coney Island. Sea Lion Park, which later changed its name to Luna Park, was the first to open at Coney Island, in 1895. Dreamland and Steeplechase Park soon followed as showmen found they could monopolize a customer's time — and money — by enclosing several attractions within a park's borders and using the pay-one-price concept. Before this time, each ride had been individually owned and operated.

This park idea caught on and spread like wildfire throughout the East Coast. Whalom Park was established in the late 1800s and has survived over the years. Situated on the picturesque shores of Lake Whalom in Lunenburg, Massachusetts, this amusement park is one of the oldest. Many amusement parks at the time were purchased by the local street railroad company; Whalom Park was bought by the Fitchburg and Leominster Street Railway Company in 1892. Local street railway companies were charged a flat rate for their power, but since this rate did not always relate to the number of riders, owners developed the parks at the end of the railway line in order to sell fares during slow periods — weeknights and weekends — to help offset the cost of power. The idea was so popular that virtually every area had one or more street railway parks.

The next step toward modern theme parks was Playland Park in Rye Beach, New York. In the mid–1920s, the Westchester County Park Commission purchased part of Rye Beach with the idea of creating a completely planned park suitable for families, much like Disney's goal in the 1950s. The commission's intent was to create an "unequaled seaside park to provide clean, wholesome recreation for people of Westchester County."

After studying other amusement parks of the day, Playland became America's first totally planned amusement park and the prototype for today's theme park. Frank W. Darling was hired to oversee the construction, and became the first manager of the park. His credentials included former manager of a Coney Island park, president of the L.A. Thompson Scenic Railway Company, and president of the National Association of Amusement Parks. It was his association with Fred Church (Traver/Church) that brought the famous Aeroplane coaster to Playland.

With the overwhelming success of Disneyland Park, after its opening in the 1950s, the planned theme park became the wave of the future and the springboard of the coaster revival. While Disneyland was prominent in reviving the roller coaster, Six Flags is perhaps more responsible for leading the revival.

Established in 1961, Six Flags' original park was located midway between Dallas and Fort Worth, Texas, on the former Waggoner DDD Ranch. The idea was to draw the bulk of its guests from within a 300-mile radius. Like Disneyland, Six Flags based its operation on a wholesome atmosphere and grounds that were kept clean. This regional theme park led to others around the country, which today are home to some of the world's greatest roller coasters.

Most modern parks contain an updated version of the famous Coney Island Scenic Railway, using tubular steel tracks instead of a wooden track. These rides were the brainchildren of Arrow Dynamics and usually took the theme of runaway mine trains. These new coasters were actually cousins to the first steel tubular tracked Matterhorn Bobsleds roller coaster at Disneyland.

Luna Park (Museum of the City of New York).

Steeplechase Park (1897–1964) (Brooklyn Public Library–Brooklyn Collection).

Arrow Dynamics was a small machine shop in northern California when it was commissioned in 1946 to build a carousel for the San Jose City Park. Arrow's work caught the eye of Walt Disney, who was impressed with the quality and craftsmanship and realized that he had found a source to help make his dream of Disneyland a reality. He bought one-third of the business that would eventually design and build an entire series of unique rides for his park including Snow White's Scary Adventures, Peter Pan's Flight, Dumbo the Flying Elephant, the Mad Hatter's Tea Party, and the Casey Jr. Circus Train.

In 1959, Arrow took its first venture into roller coasters by manufacturing Disney's Matterhorn Bobsleds ride. A true innovation in engineering and construction, the Matterhorn Bobsleds became the first modern all-steel coaster, using a tubular track and nylon wheels on the trains. This ride became the basis for a new breed of coasters and its success created a tremendous demand on Arrow by the new parks for similar rides; one of the next Arrow creations was the popular runaway mine train coasters. Steel coasters became popular because they resulted in a smooth, more silent, ride. They also enabled designers to build spirals and turns not feasible with wooden tracks. Steel coaster construction would flourish during the next few years.

In 1972, a wooden twin-track coaster called the Racer opened at Kings

Runaway Mine Train (Six Flags Over Texas).

Island just outside of Cincinnati, Ohio. Designed by John Allen, this wooden coaster played a prominent role in reviving the interest in wooden roller coasters in the United States.

John Allen created five wooden roller coasters between 1972 and 1976, each bigger and better than its predecessor. All were basically out-and-backs, a speedy design that follows a relatively straight, but undulated, path out from the station into a banked curve, and then returns back along a course roughly parallel to the first. Allen, who was associated with the Philadelphia Toboggan Company, used this pattern to emphasize speed and quick gravity shifts.

Since opening the Racer, dozens of new wooden coasters have been built, each attempting to outdo the other in height, length, and speed. This new surge has much to do with the advances made in engineering and technology.

The basic principle of a wooden roller coaster remains the same today: The train is released at the ride's highest point so as to maximize the amount of gravitational potential energy. It is this potential energy that allows the train enough momentum to coast over the entire track or until it encounters another lift hill. No hill can be higher than the initial lift since it would require more energy than the train began with. The speed is also determined by the height and slope of the first hill. Assuming a drop at a 55-degree angle, the lift hill would have to be 400 feet tall to give the train a speed of 100 miles per hour. Velocity equals the square root of two times gravity times height.

Other considerations must be addressed including wind drag and the friction between the wheels and the track. These energy losses — along with grav-

ity — must be balanced so that the train will not stop anywhere on the track other than at the loading station.

Another important consideration in designing a coaster is related to the forces it will unleash. Known as G-force or "G's," this is the pressure felt by riders as they reach the bottom of a hill and begin to climb again. On the other hand, riders feel the sensation of floating or negative G-force when the train flies over a hill, commonly referred to as "airtime."

Another force felt may be due to the curves on a track. As the train turns along a curve, there is a sideways force felt if the track has not been banked to the optimum angle. This is generally the case because of space restrictions, which call for turns to be made without the perfect angle. Many coasters are designed this way intentionally, to provide for a rougher ride.

Gone are the days of trial and error. Today, roller coaster design is a science, and designers are precise, relying on computers to help calculate the coaster's exact dimensions. Engineers feed all information into the computer to measure all potential forces upon a rider. At the turn of the century, little was known about gravity forces and the effect they had on passengers. Today, physicians are often consulted about the biomechanics of a ride and engineering and computer skills are essential in the design process.

With new technology and the introduction of steel track in the Matterhorn Bobsleds and the runaway mine trains, designers were able to create smooth, twisting courses that were mild versions of the larger wooden coasters. Many coaster buffs claimed that the smoother ride took away the excitement, however. To many, it seemed that technology was taking a step backward.

Designers then discovered that steel could be used to turn the cars upside down. The main breakthrough was the development of the corkscrew by Arrow in 1975, offering riders head-over-heels excitement as a substitute for smoothing out the sometimes bruising rides of the woodies. The steel track is made of round pipe so that the train's three sets of wheels can be contoured to fit and keep the train from falling in the unlikely event that it stops while upside down.

Coaster builders had been trying to perfect a loop since the late 1800s, but Arrow finally found the correct configuration. By changing the shape of the loop into an elliptical corkscrew, Arrow found that the G-force could be reduced to a comfortable level. The force on the ear-

lier circle loops was around 12 G's — Air Force fighter pilots can tolerate only 11 G's before blacking out! Still, when Arrow built a full-scale prototype of the corkscrew, it found a heavy G-load, but the designers' concerns were lessened when they found similar forces on the Giant Dipper, an old wooden coaster in Santa Cruz, California.

The success of the corkscrew was followed by the giant clothoid loop in 1976, a breakthrough that was independently developed by several designers. Teardrop in shape, this loop lowered the centrifugal force placed on riders because it was composed of radii of varying lengths. In a circle loop, the train would require so much speed to complete the rotation that it would place an unbearable force upon

Giant Dipper (Santa Cruz Beach Boardwalk).

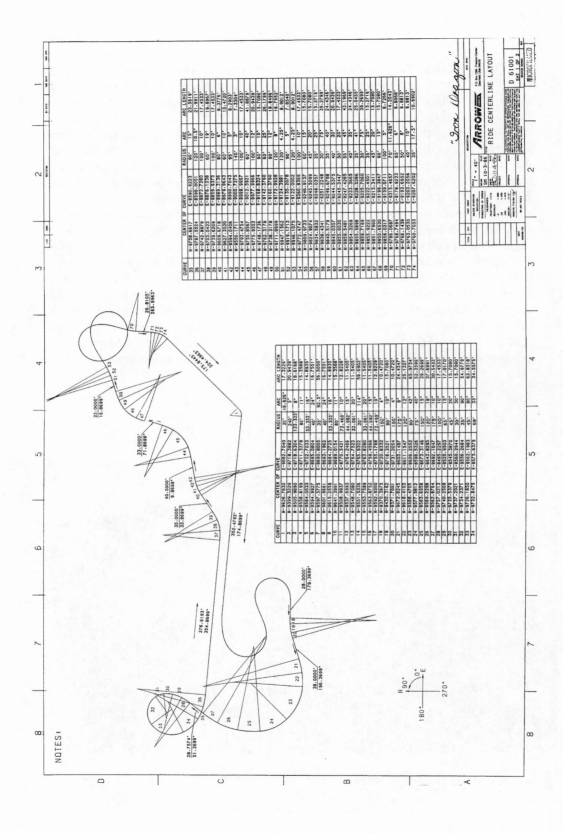

Shockwave (Paramount's Kings Dominion).

riders when entering the loop. The tremendous speed was necessary because the train would decelerate sharply as it reached the top. The teardrop shape, however, smoothes out the entry while tightening the top of the loop. This causes an acceleration that helps counteract gravity due to the smaller radius at the top; the shorter the radius, the faster the movement.

The perfection of these loops has led to practically unlimited possibilities. The limits on design today are economics but certainly not physics. When a park is thinking of installing a coaster, the main considerations are maintenance cost and public opinion. The coaster has to pay for itself by bringing people into the park.

New coasters are built each year as amusement parks around the world continue to expand. The following is a look into the development of one such ride set to open in 2000.

When Holiday World decided to build another roller coaster, they realized it would have to stand up to their highly regarded Raven. Taking advantage of the park's thickly wooded and hilly terrain within the Halloween section, Custom Coasters International began construction on the largest wooden coaster in Indiana or Kentucky.

For additional design assistance, Holiday World decided to seek the advice of the world's foremost roller coaster authority — the enthusiasts! Through the Internet, roller coaster enthusiasts from around the world were asked for their input regarding the de-

Opposite page: Iron Dragon Layout (Arrow Dynamics).

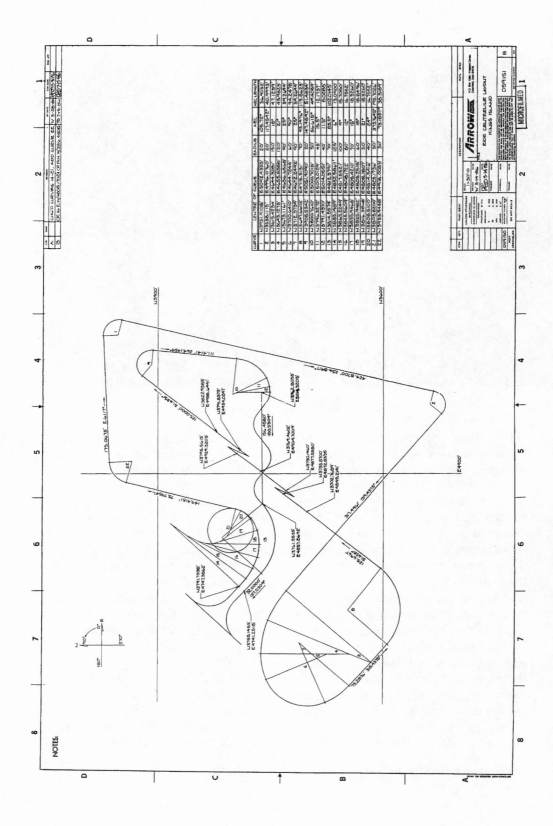

The Legend (Holiday World).

sign, theme and name. Using several suggestions, the $3 million coaster was named "The Legend" based upon a theme of "The Legend of Sleepy Hollow."

There are three major drops of 113 feet, 64 feet, plus a rare spiral drop of 77 feet and a double helix. Riders navigate 4,042 feet of track at speeds up to 68 mph, as if being chased in terror by the relentless headless horseman. Before crossing the bridge, this experience also includes four tunnels and multiple crossovers of existing attractions.

The motivating factor in the decision to invest in another wooden roller coaster came down to economics. Holiday World anticipates a 20 percent increase in attendance due to the addition of this two minute adventure.

What does the future hold? The Seventies brought back the woodie, but the steel tracks took us through corkscrews, vertical loops, and boomerangs. It took

us upside down while sitting and standing — and even suspended us below the track. Today by incorporating technology developed in the 1940s for launching rockets, roller coasters have evolved to the point that lift hills are no longer required. Premier Rides offers Linear Induction Motors that create a "magnetic river" capable of propelling a train from zero to 70 mph within four seconds. Similarly, the Linear Synchronous Motors used on Superman the Escape launched this one from zero to a record 100 mph within seven seconds.

Acknowledging the unlimited use of steel track, designers now concentrate on how positioning the rider interacts with the coaster experience. A couple of the latest developments are tiered theater-style seating and floorless seating by Bolliger & Mabillard in which riders are basically put on a pedestal. But perhaps the most extreme placement of a human being is on the "flying" coaster by

Opposite page: Vortex Layout (Arrow Dynamics).

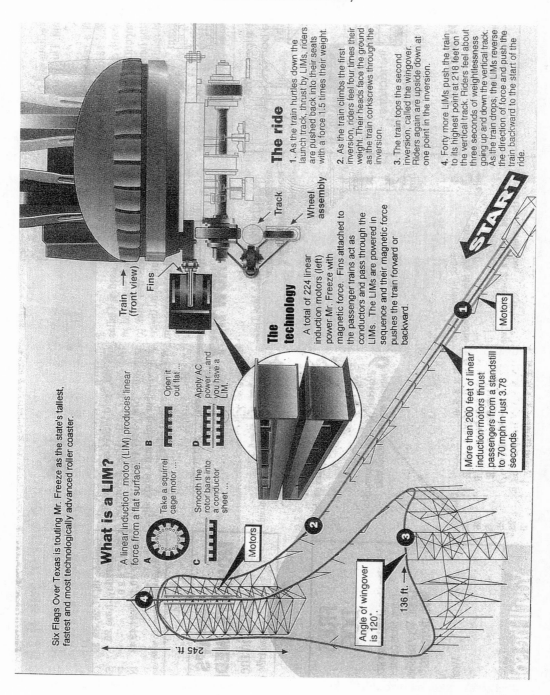

Linear Induction Motors (Premier Rides, Inc.).

LINEAR INDUCTION
CATAPULT COASTER

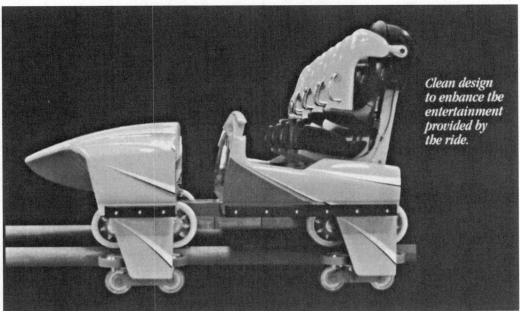

Clean design
to enhance the
entertainment
provided by
the ride.

Top: Linear Induction Catapult Coaster (Premier Rides, Inc.). *Bottom:* Kumba Coaster Car (Bolliger & Mabillard).

Oblivion 1998 at Alton Towers–England (Bolliger & Mabillard).

Vekoma. Climbing the lift, seats tilt until your back is parallel to the track followed by an inversion that leaves you in a suspended flying position.

While the steel coasters continue to challenge our imagination, nothing can take the place of a classic wooden roller coaster. Fortunately the number of woodies is beginning to increase again. Companies like Custom Coasters Inter-

Wooden close-up (Great Coasters International).

Master Blaster Water Coaster (NBGS International).

Top: Millennium Force (Cedar Point). *Bottom:* Hyper-Coaster (D. H. Morgan Manufacturing).

national and Great Coasters International have several projects on the drawing board in response to a growing demand for thrill rides that create a sense of nostalgia.

Whatever your preference, wood or steel, the future looks bright for roller coasters and their fans. From the old fashioned side-friction of Leap-the-Dips (1902) to the high-tech 310 foot tall Millennium Force (2000), there has never been a more diversified selection of roller coasters. Enjoy the ride!

Roller Coasters
in the United States

Visionland

5051 Prince Street
Bessemer, Alabama 35022-7815
www.visionlandpark.com

Opening in 1998, Alabama's first theme park is owned and operated by the West Jefferson Amusement and Public Park Authority which is a collaboration of eleven cities that helped finance this $65 million project.

Rampage (Visionland Theme Park).

RAMPAGE (1998)　A twister design by Custom Coasters International, this wooden layout is 3,500 feet long and includes eighteen crossovers and twelve turns. The 120-foot-tall lift drops trains at 56 miles per hour along a 52-degree slope.

MARVEL MANIA (1998)　This is a small steel coaster designed specifically for children.

Waterville USA
906 Gulf Shores Parkway
Gulf Shores, Alabama 36547

This is a combination of water park and "dry" park that opened in 1987.

CANNON BALL RUN (1995)　Custom Coasters International designed this wooden out-and-back with a height of 65-feet, a length of 1,700 feet and an average speed of 43 mph, topping out at 50 mph.

Castles & Coasters
9445 Metro Parkway East
Phoenix, Arizona 85051

This 13-acre park opened in 1977 as a family entertainment center offering miniature golf, go karts and an arcade. Today the only roller coasters in the state can be found here.

DESERT STORM (1993)　Built over a go-kart track, this 2,000-foot-long steel coaster begins with a 90-foot lift followed by a dive into the first of two vertical loops. Designed by O.D. Hopkins, the ride is completed by meandering back to the station.

PATRIOT (1993)　O.D. Hopkins designed this tame steel coaster as a family ride with a 35-foot high lift and 700 feet of track.

Magic Springs Theme Park
1701 E. Grand Avenue
Hot Springs, Arkansas 71901

After a two year hiatus, this 1978 amusement park reopened in 2000. Here you will find a ride with a true "roller coaster" history.

ARKANSAS TWISTER (1978)   Originally designed by Don Rosser and engineered by Bill Cobb, this 3,500-foot-long woodie began life as Roaring Tiger at Ringling Brothers and Barnum & Bailey CircusWorld in Florida. In 1986, the park converted to Boardwalk and Baseball, so consequently the name was changed to the Florida Hurricane. Then in 1990 this ride was dismantled and hauled by 29 semi-trucks to Hot Springs. Here, the reassembled coaster opened in 1992 and ran until the two year closure.

Disneyland Park
1313 Harbor Boulevard
Anaheim, California 92803
www.disneyland.com

Opened in 1955, this was the first completely planned theme park. Today there are four themed roller coasters in the park.

Matterhorn Bobsleds (© Disney Enterprises, Inc.).

Space Mountain (© **Disney Enterprises, Inc.**).

MATTERHORN BOBSLEDS (1959)   Designed by Arrow Dynamics, this was the first steel coaster using tubular tracks. The top of the Matterhorn is 146 feet high but passenger cars only reach 80 feet before spiraling down, through and around the icy mountain, finishing with a splash as the cars hit the water at the base.

SPACE MOUNTAIN (1977)   Built after the success of Space Mountain in Walt Disney World Resort, this Space Mountain is only slightly different. There is only one track and passengers sit side by side in these trains. The layout of the ride is similar to Walt Disney World Resort's but the ride is much smoother.

BIG THUNDER MOUNTAIN RAILROAD (1979)   This is the ultimate runaway mine train–type coaster. Much longer and more detailed than the others, it still uses tubular steel tracks.

GADGET'S GO COASTER (1993)   A Vekoma Roller Skater–style steel coaster 679 feet long located in Mickey's Toontown.

Big Thunder Mountain Railroad (© Disney Enterprises, Inc.).

Montezooma's Revenge (Knott's Berry Farm).

Knott's Berry Farm
8039 Beach Boulevard
Buena Park, California 90620
www.knotts.com

Knott's Berry Farm park opened in 1940 as Old West Ghost Town, near Walter

Knott's berry stand. Over the years more themed sections were added and the name was changed to Knott's Berry Farm. Today the park is owned by Cedar Fair Ltd.

MONTEZOOMA'S REVENGE (1978)　A shuttle loop–type coaster with a ride that takes a little over half a minute. It reaches 55 miles per hour before entering the 76-foot high, 360-degree loop. It then runs to the top of the 148-foot high tower before stopping and returning backwards through the loop and to the station.

BOOMERANG (1990)　Designed by Vekoma International of The Netherlands, this coaster turns riders upside down six times in less than 1 minute. First pulled backwards up to the top of a nearly eleven-story tower, the train is then released and attains 50 miles per hour, goes through a boomerang and vertical loop, then heads up another nearly vertical eleven-story tower where the whole trip begins again — backwards.

JAGUAR! (1995)　This Zierer steel coaster is designed as a smooth family ride with a top speed of 30 miles per hour. The 2,600-foot-long track has a lift height of 65 feet.

WINDJAMMER (1997)　Designed by Robin Hall and manufactured by Togo, this dual steel track racing coaster replaces the Wacky Soap Box Racers. The tracks are bright red and yellow, each with a 60-foot drop and one vertical loop. Small two car trains follow these 1,600-foot-long courses.

TIMBERLINE TWISTER (1983)　A short 488-foot-long steel children's coaster.

GHOST RIDER (1998)　Created by Custom Coaster International this wooden thriller opened on December 8th at "High Noon." The first of its kind in Knott's Berry Farm, it has a 118-foot high lift, 55 miles per hour top speed and runs over 4,600 feet of track.

LEGOLAND California
One LEGO Drive
Carlsbad, California 92008
www.lego.com

If you are familiar with the unique sound that comes from rummaging through a pile of LEGOs, this is the park of you! Opened in 1999, this place is a 128-acre tribute to the success of Acrylonitrile Butadiene Styrene (the plastic used in LEGOs) and the over 200 billion pieces that have been produced since 1949.

THE DRAGON (1999)　This roller coaster was designed as a "pink knuckle" family ride focusing on the scenic aspect of the adventure.

Bonfante Gardens Theme Park

3050 Hecker Pass Highway
Gilroy, California 95020
www.heckerpass.com

This theme park is scheduled to open in the spring of 2001 adjacent to "Hecker Pass — A Family Adventure" which is owned and operated by Michael Bonfante.

QUICKSILVER EXPRESS (2001)   This runaway mine train roller coaster is being designed and built by D.H. Morgan Manufacturing.

Quicksilver Express (Bonfante Gardens).

Scandia Screamer (Scandia Amusement Park).

Scandia Amusement Park

1155 South Wanamaker Avenue
Ontario, California 91761

Opened in 1992, this is one four Scandia parks developed by the Larson family whose Scandinavian heritage reflects the theme.

SCANDIA SCREAMER (1995) Due to space limitations, the ride was built above existing attractions and is located over one of the park's entrances. Father and son, Tony and Ty Larson designed this 2,600-foot-long, four-layer compact coaster with engineering assistance by Fred Miler. Trains consisting of six spacious two-passenger cars follow a narrow steel track that begins with a 90-foot lift and a first drop of 80 feet at 50 mph. Expect to spend a lot of time off of your seat!

Belmont Park

3126 Mission Boulevard, Suite H
San Diego, California 92109
www.belmontpark.com

Located on Mission Beach, this was once the site of an amusement park that closed in 1976. Today there are shops, restaurants, and a completely restored roller coaster, which was also closed between 1976 and August 1990. There is also a small museum and gift shop devoted to roller coaster history and trivia, where tickets for the Giant Dipper are bought.

GIANT DIPPER (1925)   The revival of this classic wood-scaffold coaster was completed in August 1990. Originally designed by the renowned team of Frank Prior and Frederick Church, this is considered to be a sister of the Giant Dipper (1924) in Santa Cruz. Although that coaster was designed by Arthur Looff, Prior and Church patents were used on its planning. The Belmont Park coaster has tighter turns with steeper banks, however.

Giant Dipper (Lee Schwabe).

Paramount's Great America
P.O. Box 1776
Santa Clara, California 95052
www.pgathrills.com

Home of the world's tallest double-decker carousel and the first "flying" coaster. Opened in 1976, this was originally one of the two Marriott theme parks. Today the park is owned and operated by Paramount Parks, a unit of Viacom Inc.

THE GRIZZLY (1986)   This is a 3,200-foot-long wooden coaster based on the Wildcat, a coaster that ran from 1911 to 1964 at Coney Island in Cincinnati, Ohio. Its highest point is 90 feet and it has a top speed of 55 miles per hour during its 2 minute, 40 second run.

GREASED LIGHTNIN' (1977)   A shuttle loop coaster that goes forward and then backward along an 849-foot-long track. The train goes from 0 to 55 miles per hour in 4.2 seconds just before entering the 76-foot high loop. Formerly known as the Tidal Wave, this Schwarzkopf design only takes 36 seconds to ride.

THE DEMON (1980)   A steel coaster by Arrow Dynamics that has a lift height of 82 feet, two vertical loops of 70 and 55 feet, and a double corkscrew. The track is 1,250 feet long with tunnels located along the way. Riding time is 1 minute, 45 seconds.

VORTEX (1991)   Designed by Bolliger & Mabillard of Switzerland, this was the first "stand-up" steel coaster west of the Mississippi. On this 2-minute ride, passengers stand instead of sit as they follow a 1,920-foot track at 45 mph with the highlight being a 360-degree vertical loop.

INVERTIGO (1998)   This was the first inverted, suspended boomerang in North America designed by Vekoma. The layout is similar to other boomerangs but on this ride you sit face-to-face, suspended under the track for the one and a half minute duration.

GREEN SLIME MINE CAR (1987)   Renamed in 1995 in conjunction with the Nickelodeon Splat City section, this Intamin designed children's steel coaster is 1,300 feet long and runs for two minutes.

TAXI JAM (1999)   A 288-foot-long children's steel coaster designed by Miler Coaster Company. This one minute experience is a terrific initiation for the young novice.

TOP GUN (1993)   Bolliger & Mabillard designed this inverted coaster, which suspends the riders below the track. From a 100-foot lift the train takes off at 50 miles per hour along 2,260 feet of track, going upside down on the outside of a vertical loop and corkscrew. The entire ride lasts 2 minutes, 26 seconds.

The Grizzly (Paramount's Great America).

Greased Lightnin' (Paramount's Great America).

The Demon (Paramount's Great America).

Invertigo (Paramount's Great America).

"PROJECT STEALTH" (2000)   This prototype coaster by Vekoma has been referred to as a "flying" or "laydown" coaster. Boarding in an upright position, four "seats" across in six rows, the seats tilt until your back is against the track. At the top of the 115-foot lift, the track inverts, leaving riders in a "flying" position. From there you glide along 2,766 feet of track for 1 minute and 50 seconds at speeds up to 50 mph, encountering one vertical loop, a double corkscrew and a horseshoe curve.

Santa Cruz Beach Boardwalk
400 Beach Street
Santa Cruz, California 95060
www.beachboardwalk.com

In bygone days, the Pacific Coast sported a string of boardwalks and amusement facilities. Then, one by one, the Pike in Long Beach, Playland in San Francisco, parks in Venice, Santa Monica, Portland, and San Diego, and the roller coasters these parks featured all disappeared. Santa Cruz became a tourist attraction in 1865, when John Liebrandt built the first of many public bathhouses near the mouth of the San Lorenzo River. Bathhouse owners preached the health benefits of bathing in salt water to attract

California

Taxi Jam (Paramount's Great America).

Top Gun (Paramount's Great America).

Giant Dipper (Santa Cruz Beach Boardwalk).

increasing numbers of tourists, who streamed into Santa Cruz using these facilities to change into swimsuits and enjoy the ocean's "natural medicine." Soon, concessions and a boardwalk patterned after the ones at Coney Island sprang up nearby. Today you can still grab the brass ring on their classic Merry-Go-Round.

GIANT DIPPER (1924)   Built in just 47 days at a cost of $50,000 this coaster is ½ mile long, a classic wooden twister, with graceful arches and sweeping fan curves that are surpassed only by the terror of its 70-foot drop and 55 miles per hour speeds. This structure was designed by Arthur Looff, who envisioned a giant wooden roller coaster that would be a "combination of earthquake, balloon ascension, and aeroplane drop." In 1987, the Giant Dipper was honored as a National Historic Landmark by the U.S. National Park Service.

HURRICANE (1992)   German designed and manufactured in Italy, this S. D. C. Windstorm steel coaster has a compact layout, which allows it to fit into the limited space of the boardwalk. It is described as unusually smooth for a coaster of its size, with 80-degree banked turns and twisting dives. The only other one like it in the United States is located in Long Island's Adventureland.

Hurricane (Santa Cruz Beach Boardwalk).

Hurricane (Santa Cruz Beach Boardwalk).

Six Flags Magic Mountain

P.O. Box 5500
Valencia, California 91355
www.sixflags.com

The Six Flags Magic Mountain park opened in 1971 and is now owned by Premier Parks Inc.

VIPER (1990)   Designed by Arrow, this 3,830-foot-long ride is the world's largest looping steel roller coaster. It features three 360-degree loops, a double barrel boomerang, a classic corkscrew, and an eighteen-story drop with speeds reaching 70 miles per hour, all during a 2½ minute time span.

NINJA (1988)   The first and only suspended coaster on the West Coast. Arrow designed this 2,700-foot-long, 2 minute ride with angles up to 180 degrees and speeds of 55 miles per hour.

REVOLUTION (1976)   The world's first giant looping roller coaster. Revolution is a smooth 3,457-foot-long steel ride with one 360-degree vertical loop and a 144-foot long tunnel, designed by Anton Schwarzkopf. The 2½ minute ride has a top speed of 55 miles per hour and G-forces of 4.94 when entering the loop.

Viper (Six Flags Magic Mountain).

COLOSSUS (1978)   At a top height of 115 feet, this is one of the tallest, longest, and fastest dual-track wooden roller coasters in the world. Designed by International Amusement Devices, Inc., the track is 4,325 feet long and has 14 hills that are covered in 3½ minutes at a top speed of 62 miles per hour.

GOLD RUSHER (1971)   A runaway mine train–type roller coaster designed by Arrow Dynamics.

PSYCLONE (1991)   This is a classic wooden replica of the famous Coney Island Cyclone, designed by Curtis D. Summers. It begins with a 95-foot, 53-degree angled first drop and continues with five fan-banked turns, ten more drops and a 183-foot long tunnel. The total ride takes 1 minute, 50 seconds, and the fastest speed is 50 miles per hour.

FLASHBACK (1985)   This compact steel coaster designed by Intamin was originally built for Six Flags Great America, where it operated until 1988; then at Six Flags Over Georgia until 1991. It has a unique design that simulates flight by making six quick-turning vertical dives over a 1,900-foot-long track. From a lift height of 86 feet, the train can reach speeds of 35 miles per hour during its 1½ minute run.

BATMAN: THE RIDE (1994)   Designed by Bolliger & Mabillard, this inverted coaster is 2,700-feet long and includes two vertical outside loops and a twisting "Heartline Spin." From a 100-foot lift, the suspended train

Revolution (Six Flags Magic Mountain).

Ninja (Six Flags Magic Mountain).

Colossus (Six Flags Magic Mountain).

Psyclone (Six Flags Magic Mountain).

Flashback (Six Flags Magic Mountain).

begins a 2 minute, 50 mile per hour ride, through an area themed for Batman: The Movie.

THE RIDDLER'S REVENGE (1998)   This 4,370-foot-long coaster that you can ride while standing is designed by Bolliger & Mabillard. From a height of 156 feet the train travels 65 mph through six inversions including a record high, 124-foot, 360-degree vertical loop.

SUPERMAN: THE ESCAPE (1997)   Called the world's tallest, fastest and most technologically advanced thrill ride, this may or may not be a roller coaster, but its linear synchronous motors (LSM) have opened the door to a new wave of coasters that use a system called Linear Induction Motors (LIM). With these magnetic propellents, the 6 ton, 15 seat vehicles on Superman can go from 0 to 100 mph in 7 seconds before heading straight up the 415-foot tower for a 6.5 second weightless experience.

Six Flags Marine World
2001 Marine World Parkway
Vallejo, California 94589-4006
www.sixflags.com

Flashback (Six Flags Magic Mountain).

Top: Batman:The Ride (Six Flags Magic Mountain). Bottom: The Riddler's Revenge (Six Flags Magic Mountain).

Opened in 1968 as an Oceanarium, today Marine World has expanded into a full-fledged theme park as part of the Premier Parks family.

KONG (1998) This inverted Vekoma coaster sits riders in rows of two with feet dangling below. Up a 115-foot lift and diving to within inches of the ground on the first drop the ride begins to cover its 5 inversions along 2,172 feet of track.

ROAR (1999) Great Coasters International starts this wooden thriller with a lift of 95 feet that leads to a 50-degree, 50-mph plunge into a 133-degree right turn. Other highlights of the 3,467-foot-long track are the 22 crossovers, 17 turns, 10 reversals and 12 drops resulting in 12 points of weightlessness.

THE BOOMERANG (1998) Having reached the second 125-foot tower, the train is released again, backward, to follow the track through 3 inversions in reverse. Another Vekoma Boomerang.

ROAD RUNNER EXPRESS (1999) A smaller figure-eight steel roller coaster for the beginners...only 14 feet off the ground.

Kong (Six Flags Marine World).

Roar (Six Flags Marine World).

Lakeside
4601 Sheridan Boulevard
Denver, Colorado 80212

Opened in 1908, Lakeside is a traditional amusement park that comes alive at night with colorful neon patterns. Among the attractions is a small gauge steam train that originally operated at the 1904 World's Fair in St. Louis, Missouri.

THE CYCLONE (1940)   A traditional wooden coaster designed by Ed Vettal. From a 90-foot tall lift, it takes just under 2 minutes to complete this 2,800-foot-long twisting and turning track.

WILD CHIPMUNK (1955)   This "Mad Mouse"–style coaster zig-zags over 1,150 feet of steel track at 21 mph from a 41-foot elevation.

DRAGON (1989)   Zamperla designed this 280-foot-long kiddie coaster.

Six Flags Elitch Gardens
299 Walnut St.
Denver, Colorado 80204-1887
www.sixflags.com

The Boomerang (Six Flags Marine World).

John and Mary Elitch opened their garden to the public in 1890, with P.T. Barnum and General and Mrs. Tom Thumb on hand for the festivities. In 1995 the park reopened at its new spacious downtown location. Today this amusement park is owned by Premier Parks and is a member of the Six Flags Family.

TWISTER II (1995)   Rather than relocate the 30-year-old P.T.C. classic, Elitch's elected to construct a new twister. Designed by John Pierce, this wooden roller coaster is 4,640 feet long, 100 feet high and has a top speed of 55 mph.

SIDEWINDER (1980)   Moved to this park in 1995, the single vertical loop is the highlight of this Arrow designed steel shuttle loop. The train is propelled from the station and returns backwards along the 653-foot-long track.

WILD KITTEN (1995)   This is a 100-foot-long children's steel coaster designed by Allen Herschell.

BOOMERANG COAST TO COASTER (1999)   Covering approximately 1,800 feet of track, forward and backward at 50 mph, this Vekoma coaster encounters three inversions.

THE MIND ERASER (1997)   Another Vekoma steel coaster that suspends passengers under the 2,172-foot long track and travels at 60 mph. This 100-foot tall ride not only has a minimum height restriction of 52 inches, but also a maximum clearance of 80 inches due to the hanging seat positions.

Lake Compounce
822 Lake Avenue
Bristol, Connecticut 06010
www.lakecompounce.com

Opened to the public in 1846 with walking paths, a bandstand, picnic tables, and rowboats, a trolley line was brought to the park in 1896. The first coaster was built in 1914 (Green Dragon) but was replaced in 1927. In 1996, the Kennywood Entertainment Company became the managing partner of this park.

THE WILDCAT (1927)   Built by the Philadelphia Toboggan Company, this coaster is a classic example of the Golden Age of coaster architecture. It was completely refurbished in 1985 by Charles Dinn. The deteriorated wood was replaced, board for board, with pressure treated, long leaf yellow pine, and 3,000 feet of steel-banded track. Though a small coaster by today's standards, the combination of wood and two high-bank fan curves makes for a fast-paced, intense ride. The first drop is 78–80 feet high and the riding time is only 52 seconds.

The Wildcat (Lake Compounce).

BOULDER DASH (2000)   Taking advantage of the natural terrain, Custom Coasters International designed this wooden thriller to initially drop 115 feet at 60 mph with an overall drop of 140 feet. The 4,500 feet of track is built on the mountainside among the rocks, boulders, cliffs and ledges which form the western boundary of the park.

Old Town

5770 W. Irlo Bronson Memorial Hwy
Kissimmee, Florida 34746
www.old-town.com

Old Town is a free admission entertainment complex featuring specialty stores, restaurants and amusement attractions. Among the 15 rides is the very first "Scrambler," produced in 1944.

WINDSTORM (1997) Manufactured by Zamperla, Inc., of Italy, this 1,437-foot-long steel coaster is a high banking, twisting 35 mph ride with a 60-foot height and a compact footprint.

Walt Disney World Resort

P.O. Box 10100
Lake Buena Vista, Florida 32830-0100
www.waltdisneyworld.com

Windstorm (Old Town).

Opened in October of 1971, this complete resort includes the Magic Kingdom, Epcot, the Disney-MGM Studios and Disney's Animal Kingdom among its many parks.

Magic Kingdom:

SPACE MOUNTAIN (1975) Located in the Tomorrowland section of the Magic Kingdom, this cone shaped structure rises to a height of 183 feet and encompasses 4,508,500 cubic feet of dark mysterious space. Passengers board rocket shuttles that climb high into space before beginning the descent along 3,000 feet of intricate twisting track.

BIG THUNDER MOUNTAIN RAILROAD (1980) This is the ultimate runaway type of roller coaster. Each train carries up to thirty passengers along 2,780 feet of track, past sandstone buttes and windswept canyons, through a booming gold rush, and into big thunder mine.

THE BARNSTORMER (1996) This themed steel coaster is a Vekoma "roller skater" family ride. The track is 679 feet long and the train is designed to look like bi-planes.

Disney-MGM Studios:

ROCK 'N' ROLLER COASTER STARRING AEROSMITH (1999) With the assistance of Linear Induction Motors, the "Limo" shaped trains are launched to 60 mph in 2.8 seconds. Surrounded by rock-concert lighting and synchronized to a specially created Aerosmith soundtrack blasting from 120 onboard speakers, this indoor coaster follows 3,400 feet of Vekoma track through 3 inversions and a series of drops and turns.

SeaWorld Adventure Park

7007 Seaworld Drive
Orlando, Florida 32821
www.4adventure.com

Established in 1973, SeaWorld is a 135-acre theme park dedicated to marine life. With the Busch Entertainment Corporation as the current owner, several new attractions have been added, including themed thrill rides.

KRAKEN (2000) Named for the mythological sea monster, riders sit on an open-sided pedestal with legs dangling above the track, essentially "floorless."

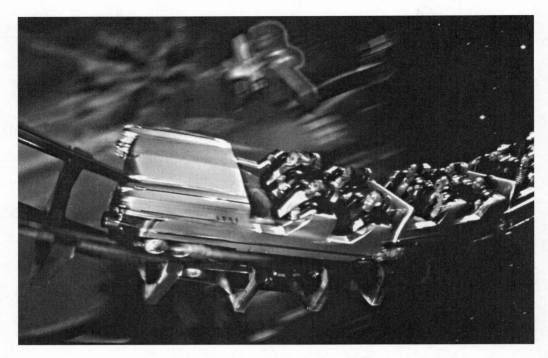

Rock 'n' Roller Coaster (© Disney Enterprises, Inc.).

The second of its kind designed by Bolliger & Mabillard, there is a 144-foot first drop and 4,177 feet of track with seven inversions and three underwater plunges. Top speed during this 3 minute, 39 second, adventure is 65 mph.

Universal Studios Escape
1000 Universal Studios Plaza
Orlando, Florida 32819-7601
www.universalstudios.com

This destination resort includes the Universal Studios Florida theme park which opened in 1990, the City Walk entertainment complex, five themed hotels and the Islands of Adventure which opened in 1999.

DUELING DRAGONS (1999)   Designed by Bolliger & Mabillard, this is the world's first inverted dueling roller coaster. The two trains share a common 125-foot lift but from there they follow their unique 3,200-foot-long tracks, experiencing several near misses with one another. From the initial lift, Fire Dragon drops 105 feet at 60 mph and the Ice Dragon drops

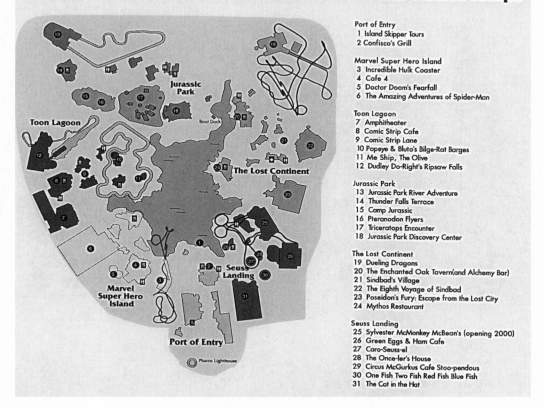

Universal Studios Islands of Adventure℠ at Universal Studios Escape℠

Port of Entry
1 Island Skipper Tours
2 Confisco's Grill

Marvel Super Hero Island
3 Incredible Hulk Coaster
4 Cafe 4
5 Doctor Doom's Fearfall
6 The Amazing Adventures of Spider-Man

Toon Lagoon
7 Amphitheater
8 Comic Strip Cafe
9 Comic Strip Lane
10 Popeye & Bluto's Bilge-Rat Barges
11 Me Ship, The Olive
12 Dudley Do-Right's Ripsaw Falls

Jurassic Park
13 Jurassic Park River Adventure
14 Thunder Falls Terrace
15 Camp Jurassic
16 Pteranodon Flyers
17 Triceratops Encounter
18 Jurassic Park Discovery Center

The Lost Continent
19 Dueling Dragons
20 The Enchanted Oak Tavern(and Alchemy Bar)
21 Sindbad's Village
22 The Eighth Voyage of Sindbad
23 Poseidon's Fury: Escape from the Lost City
24 Mythos Restaurant

Seuss Landing
25 Sylvester McMonkey McBean's (opening 2000)
26 Green Eggs & Ham Cafe
27 Caro-Seuss-el
28 The Once-ler's House
29 Circus McGurkus Cafe Stoo-pendous
30 One Fish Two Fish Red Fish Blue Fish
31 The Cat in the Hat

Map of Park (Universal Studios).

95 feet at 55 mph. Both encounter five inversions and run for approximately two and a half minutes.

THE INCREDIBLE HULK COASTER (1999)   Instead of a conventional lift, Bolliger & Mabillard used several drivewheels to accelerate the train up through a 150-foot-long tunnel in just three seconds. At this point riders immediately experience a zero–G heartline inversion and are turned upside down 110 feet above the ground followed by a 60 mph, 105-foot drop. In all, there are seven inversions during this 2 minute 15 second ride.

PTERANODON FLYERS (1999)   A suspended coaster of sorts with two swinging seats attached to the underside of each Pteranodon (a flying dinosaur). This ride glides over the treetops of a prehistoric jungle at heights up to 40 feet.

Dueling Dragons (Universal Studios).

The Incredible Hulk Coaster (Universal Studios).

WOODY WOODPECKER'S NUTHOUSE COASTER (1999)   The first roller coaster located at the studio portion of this complex is a customized Vekoma family coaster.

Miracle Strip Amusement Park
12000 Front Beach Road
Panama City, Florida 32407
www.miraclestrippark.com

Located on the Gulf of Mexico, this amusement park first opened in 1963. Today the park offers a variety of rides and live shows.

STARLINER (1963)   John Allen designed the wooden out-and-back, providing a classic backdrop for this seaside park. With a 65-foot drop from the 70-foot lift, riders are released at 55 mph to coast over 2,640 feet of track including a strategically placed tunnel.

Busch Gardens
3605 Bougainvillea Avenue
Tampa, Florida 33612
www.buschgardens.com

One of the Anheuser-Busch companies, this park is themed and dedicated to animal wildlife. Among the many attractions are four exciting steel coasters and a huge double wooden one.

PYTHON (1976)   This is a 1,250-foot-long classic tubular steel corkscrew designed by Arrow Dynamics. The train can reach a top speed of 50 miles per hour at the bottom of a 70-foot drop before entering the double corkscrew at 27 miles per hour. The complete ride takes 1 minute, 10 seconds.

SCORPION (1981)   This is an Anton Schwarzkopf coaster that rides for 2 minutes, 15 seconds. The 1,805-foot-long steel track has a first lift of 65 feet and a drop of 62 feet giving it a speed of 50 miles per hour before entering the one vertical loop. In this loop a person feels the pull of 3.5 G's.

Python (Busch Gardens, Tampa).

Scorpion (Busch Gardens, Tampa).

Kumba (Busch Gardens, Tampa).

Top: Montu (Busch Entertainment Corporation). Bottom: Gwazi (Busch Entertainment Corporation).

Gwazi (Busch Entertainment Corporation).

KUMBA (1993)   Sitting four across, passengers plunge into one of the world's largest vertical loops — 108 feet high — from a 143-foot-high lift. Bolliger & Mabillard designed this 2 minute, 54 second ride, which covers 3,978 feet of track at speeds of 60 miles per hour. The name "Kumba" means "roar" in the African Congo language, which is appropriate for this looping, spiraling coaster that at times pulls 3.75 G's.

MONTU (1996)   Designed by Bolliger & Mabillard, this inverted steel coaster begins with a 150-foot-high lift that leads to speeds in excess of 60 mph. Along the 3983 feet of track, Montu encounters 7 inversions including an "Immelman," a first-ever inverse diving loop (named after a German stunt pilot).

GWAZI (1999)   Named after a fabled lion with a tiger's head, Gwazi is actually two distinct wooden coasters intertwined. Designed by Great Coasters International, each 3,400-foot-long track duels the other with six "flyby" maneuvers in which trains pass within feet of the other at crossing speeds of 100 mph. The adrenaline begins to flow at the top of the 90-foot lift hills when both trains drop on a precise "stringline," allowing riders to see the opposite train charging straight toward them. As they hurtle down, one track veers left, the other to the right.

Six Flags Over Georgia
P.O. Box 43187
Atlanta, Georgia 30378
www.sixflags.com

This park opened around 1967 just to the west of Atlanta as the second of several parks that the company now operates.

GEORGIA CYCLONE (1990)   Designed by Curtis D. Summers, this is a twister-type coaster patterned after the legendary Coney Island Cyclone. With a 95-foot lift and a 78½-foot drop at a 53-degree angle, this coaster twists inside and out, while racing around high-banked turns along the 2,970-foot-long course. It has been described as a 10-acre ride on a 3-acre site, all packed into 1 minute, 48 seconds.

THE GREAT AMERICAN SCREAM MACHINE (1973)   This is a 3,800-foot-long wooden out-and-back designed by John Allen of the Philadelphia To-

Georgia Cyclone (Six Flags Over Georgia).

Top: The Great American Scream Machine (Six Flags Over Georgia). Bottom: Mind Bender (Six Flags Over Georgia).

Top: Ninja (Six Flags Over Georgia). Bottom: The Georgia Scorcher (Six Flags Over Georgia).

The Georgia Scorcher (Six Flags Over Georgia).

boggan Company. The first drop is 87 feet from a 105-foot-high lift. The ride takes 2 minutes.

MIND BENDER (1978)   The first triple-looping steel coaster in North America. Designed by Anton Schwarzkopf, this ride takes 2 minutes, 33 seconds, and has a lift hill of 80 feet followed by vertical loops that are 56 feet tall.

NINJA (1989)   This 2,900-foot-long, 122-foot-high steel coaster was formerly the Kamikaze at Hunts Pier, located in New Jersey until 1992. It has five inversions: corkscrew, sidewinder, and butterfly loop in a compact layout designed by Vekoma.

VIPER (1980)   A shuttle loop designed by Schwarzkopf that shoots riders through a 360-degree loop, up a 70-degree incline and then back again. This 876-foot-long coaster was relocated here in 1995 from Six Flags Astroworld in Houston, Texas.

BATMAN: THE RIDE (1997)   Bolliger & Mabillard designed this 2,693-foot-long inverted steel coaster. Ski lift–style trains, suspended from the track, dangle passengers on the outside of several inversions including a zero gravity heartline spin during the 2 minute run.

THE GEORGIA SCORCHER (1999)   One of the world's tallest (107 feet) and fastest (54 mph) stand-up roller coasters. From a first drop of 101 feet, Bolliger & Mabillard twist, turn, spiral and loop 3,000 feet of track for 2 minutes, 30 seconds.

DAHLONEGA MINE TRAIN (1967)   Developed by Arrow, this 2,323-foot-long runaway mine train is themed for the early Gold Rush days in the northern Georgia town of Dahlonega. As a sidenote, it was in reference to this location that the statement, "There's gold in them thar hills," was made.

Lake Winnepesaukah Amusement Park
Lakeview Drive
Rossville, Georgia 30741
www.lakewinnie.com

Family owned and operated since 1925, "Lake Winnie" is located just outside of

Chattanooga over the Tennessee border. This 100-acre park is as traditional as they come. Take a splash into the lake on the historic in-house designed boat chute.

> **CANNON BALL** (1967)   Designed by John Allen of the Philadelphia Toboggan Company, this 2,272-foot-long wooden out-and-back has a 70-foot lift hill which descends at a 45-degree angle. During the 1 minute, 30 second ride, the train reaches a top speed of 50 mph.

Wild Adventures
3766 Old Clyattville Road
Valdosta, Georgia 31601
www.wild-adventure.com

Opened in 1996, this park is located halfway between Atlanta and Orlando off of I-75. Wild Adventures is a combination of a zoological habitat exhibit and thrill ride park.

> **BOOMERANG** (1998)   For 1 minute and 45 seconds, this Vekoma design sends you forward and then backward through three inversions along 875-feet of track at speeds up to 50 mph.

> **TIGER TERROR** (1998)   Manufactured by Wisdom Industries, this two minute steel roller coaster ride is one for the entire family, especially the children.

> **THE HANGMAN** (1995)   Relocated here in 1999 from Opryland USA, this is a 2,172-foot-long steel suspended roller coaster with seven inversions. With feet dangling, the drop from a 120-foot lift begins this 1 minute, 30 second journey at 60 mph.

> **GOLD RUSH** (1999)   A steel Chance children's coaster that runs for 1 minute, 45 seconds at a high speed of 10 miles per hour.

> **ROLLER SKATER** (2000)   This junior roller coaster is 28 feet tall with 679 feet of steel track as designed by Vekoma.

Cannon Ball (Lake Winnepesaukah).

Silverwood Theme Park

26225 N-Highway 95
Athol, Idaho 83801
www.silverwood4fun.com

This park is the home of the first coaster to successfully take riders upside down in the modern era.

GRAVITY DEFYING CORKSCREW (1975)   Moved here in 1990 from Knott's Berry Farm, this is Arrow Dynamics' original corkscrew coaster. The 1 minute, 10 second ride begins with a 70-foot-high lift and covers 1,250 feet of track while at times reaching speeds of 45 miles per hour.

THE TIMBER TERROR (1996)   Designed by Custom Coaster Internationals, this wooden out-and-back is 2,700 feet long, has an initial lift of 85 feet and drops at 55 mph.

TREMORS (1999)   Plummeting down the first drop of 103 feet at 60 mph and into the tunnel below, the train resurfaces by bursting through the floor and roof of a gift shop. This is the first of five underground experiences incorporated into CCI's 3,000-foot-long wooden coaster.

Six Flags Great America

P.O. Box 1776
Gurnee, Illinois 60031
www.sixflags.com

Great America opened in 1976 and was one of two amusement parks owned by Marriott Corporation. The park is now part of the Six Flags family owned by Premier Parks.

SHOCKWAVE (1988)   Designed by Arrow Dynamics, this steel coaster starts at a height of 170 feet and moves down a 155-foot, 55-degree angle banking drop into a total of seven loops. It contains two 116-foot and one 130-foot vertical high loops, a double corkscrew, and a boomerang. It takes about 2 minutes, 20 seconds to cover the 3,900-foot long track with a top speed of 65 miles per hour.

THE AMERICAN EAGLE (1981)   Twin wooden racing coaster designed by Intamin, Inc. Each track is 4,650 feet long and has a lift of 127 feet. The

Gravity Defying Corkscrew (Silverwood Theme Park).

Shockwave (Six Flags Great America).

first drop is at a 55-degree angle and the top recorded speed is 66.32 miles per hour.

THE DEMON (1976)   A steel coaster by Arrow Dynamics that was modified in 1980. It has a height of 82 feet, two vertical loops of 70 and 55 feet in height, and a double corkscrew. The track is 2,300 feet long with three mysterious tunnels. Riding time is 1 minute, 45 seconds.

IRON WOLF (1990)   By Bolliger & Mabillard, this is one of the world's largest and fastest "stand-up" looping coaster. Riders stand instead of sitting as they are propelled through more than a half mile of track packed with steep drops, two tight curves, and two 360-degree loops. It is 100 feet high, 2,900 feet long with a 90-foot first drop. It has a top speed of 55 miles per hour and a ride time of 2 minutes.

BATMAN: THE RIDE (1992)   Designed by Bolliger & Mabillard, this 2,700-foot-long prototype is the world's first inverted outside looping roller coaster. Because the cars are not allowed to swing like that of a traditional suspended coaster, it was possible to take vertical loops on the "outside" of the loop. In fact, there are a total of five inversions: two vertical loops, two flatspins (corkscrews), and a unique heart-linespin that is a roll designed to give the sensation of 0 G's for about 4 seconds. Statistically, the coaster has a high point of 100 feet, a vertical loop of 77 feet, and speeds

The American Eagle (Six Flags Great America).

The Demon (Six Flags Great America).

Iron Wolf (Six Flags Great America).

up to 50 miles per hour during the 2 minute ride. Another unique characteristic is the chair lift–type seat where your feet dangle below, as if you are on a swing. To market this new coaster concept, the name was chosen by Six Flags (Time Warner) to coincide with the Warner Bros. movie release of *Batman Returns*.

Top: Batman: The Ride (Six Flags Great America). Bottom: Viper (Six Flags Great America).

VIPER (1995)   This wooden twister was built in-house and covers 3,458 feet of track within two minutes. The top speed is 50 mph from a lift hill of 100 feet.

RAGING BULL (1999)   Referred to as one of the world's first steel hyper coasters, Bolliger & Mabillard designed this one with six inclined turns. The initial drop is 200 feet at 65 degrees (73 mph) into an underground tunnel, covering 5,057 feet of track in two and a half minutes.

Raging Bull (Six Flags Great America).

Indiana Beach
5224 East Indiana Beach Road
Monticello, Indiana 47960
www.indianabeach.com

Opened in 1926, this is a large traditional amusement park located on beautiful Lake Shafer. Stay at the camp resort and take a stroll on the Boardwalk at night.

HOOSIER HURRICANE (1994)   Space restraints becoming a factor, this wooden out-and-back was built on concrete pilings over Lake Shafer. For one minute, thirty seconds, the 3,000 feet of track takes you on a hilly ride that includes a 97-foot lift and a 94-foot first drop at 50 mph. The design is by Custom Coaster International.

TIG'RR (1981)   This compact steel twister is a Schwarzkopf Jet Star with 1,766 feet of track.

Holiday World
P.O. Box 179
Santa Claus, Indiana 47579
www.holidayworld.com

Hoosier Hurricane (Dave Wynn).

Hoosier Hurricane (Dave Wynn).

Developed by Louis J. Koch as a retirement project in 1946, Santa Claus Land has blossomed into Holiday World (1984). With the addition of major attractions and new themed sections this friendly park is more popular than ever.

THE RAVEN (1995)   Designed by Custom Coasters International, this 2,800-foot-long wooden coaster sends riders through 90 seconds of unexpected twists and turns. From a 110-foot height, at 60 mph trains encounter a 120-foot-long tunnel, 85-foot and 61-foot drops, a sharp turn over a lake and a double banked curve at the bottom of the second hill.

THE HOWLER (1999)   A family roller coaster with a single, six car train which accommodates twelve riders, designed by Zamperla.

THE LEGEND (2000)   Statistically, this wooden coaster has a maximum height of 116 feet which drops 113 feet at approximately 68 mph leading to the second drop, spiraling down 77 feet. With one more drop of 64 feet and a double helix, this two minute ride was designed by Custom Coasters International to take advantage of the hilly, wooded terrain.

The Raven (Holiday World).

The Legend (Holiday World).

Arnolds Park

P.O. Box 609
U.S. Highway 71
Arnolds Park, Iowa 51331
www.arnoldspark.com

On the shores of Lake Okoboji, W.B. Arnold established this amusement park in 1889 with the introduction of Chute-the-Chutes at his homestead. The first roller coaster was the Thriller in 1912 followed by an eventual replacement in 1927. The park closed for a year in 1987 but was reopened in time for a centennial celebration with a completely refurbished "Legend."

LEGEND (1927)   Designed by John Miller, this classic wooden out-and-back took 200 men two years to build. The length of the coaster is 1,640 feet, and the 65-foot lift hill, also known as the "Point of No Return," drops riders at 41 miles per hour.

Adventureland

P.O. Box 3355
Des Moines, Iowa 50316

Tornado (Adventureland).

Dragon (Adventureland).

The Outlaw (Adventureland).

Originally set to open in 1974, a tornado's damage delayed the first full season to 1975. The park is themed on the history of Iowa, including a turn-of-the-century main street full of architectural replicas.

TORNADO (1979)   From a 93-foot-high lift, this 2,840-foot-long coaster can reach 58 miles per hour during its 2 minute out-and-back run. This wooden coaster was designed by William Cobb.

DRAGON (1990)   O.D. Hopkins Associates, Inc., built this 2,250-foot-long double-looping coaster. It has a 90-foot-high lift with an 85-foot drop and runs for 1 minute, 30 seconds.

THE OUTLAW (1993)   The 2,600-foot-long wooden twister designed by Custom Coasters, Inc., incorporates nine drops and twelve turns in its course. The highest point is the 67-foot-high lift.

SUPER SCREAMER (1976)   A steel Galaxi style coaster with two car trains.

UNDERGROUND (1996)   An enclosed wooden coaster, 980 feet long, designed by Custom Coasters International.

Joyland
2801 South Hillside Street
Wichita, Kansas 67216

A 55-acre, family owned and operated traditional amusement park that was established in 1949.

ROLLER COASTER (1949)   The original roller coaster of this park is a wooden L-shaped out-and-back by the Philadelphia Toboggan Company, standing 80 feet high and 2,600 feet long. Herbert Schmeck designed this one minute, thirty second ride to feature "airtime."

Six Flags Kentucky Kingdom
937 Phillips Lane
P.O. Box 9287
Louisville, Kentucky 40209-0287
www.sixflags.com

Opened in 1990 at the edge of the Kentucky Fair & Exposition Center, this 55-acre amusement park becomes an integral function of the annual fair. Acquired by Premier Parks, Kentucky Kingdom became a member of the Six Flags family in 1998.

VAMPIRE (1990)   One of Vekoma's boomerangs with six inversions along 875 feet of track, three forward and three in reverse. This one minute ride has a top speed of 48 mph.

THUNDER RUN (1990)   Designed by Curtis D. Summers, this wooden whiteknuckler is 2,850 feet long with an overall height of 89 feet. At the bottom of the first drop, going 53 mph, the train does a U-turn on the 70-degree banked track instead of immediately climbing the customary "next hill."

ROLLER SKATER (1994)   This is a 679-foot-long steel family roller coaster designed by Vekoma.

T² (1995)   "Terror to the second power" is a suspended looping steel coaster with five inversions. From a 115-foot lift hill, the train drops at 60 mph and travels 2,170 feet of track designed by Vekoma.

CHANG (1997)   Bolliger & Mabillard designed this coaster as the world's tallest on which passengers have to stand while navigating 4,155 feet of track. The ride begins with a climb up a 154-foot lift hill only to be dropped 144 feet at 63 mph into a 121-foot vertical loop, the first of five inversions.

Vampire (John Nation).

Top: Thunder Run (Six Flags Kentucky Kingdom). Bottom: Roller Skater (Six Flags Kentucky Kingdom).

T² (Fieldhouse Photography).

Chang (Fieldhouse Photography).

Twisted Sisters (Fieldhouse Photography).

TWISTED SISTERS (1998)   The world's first "dueling" coaster is two wooden tracks with a combined length of 5,281 feet laid over a steel support structure. Designed by Custom Coasters, each of these tracks has a height of 75 feet and a top speed of 55 mph.

Jazzland Theme Park
P.O. Box 870250
New Orleans, Louisiana 70187-0250
www.jazzland2000.com

Opening in 2000, this 140-acre theme park is dedicated to the culture of Louisiana including a nostalgic recreation of the famed Pontchartrain Beach Amusement Park. Jazzland is owned and operated by Ogden Entertainment.

WILD MOUSE (2000)   These popular mouse coasters are well known for sudden directional changes. The swift hairpin turns are followed by a series of abrupt dips ... hang on!

BOOMERANG (2000)   Designed by Vekoma, this 875-foot-long steel

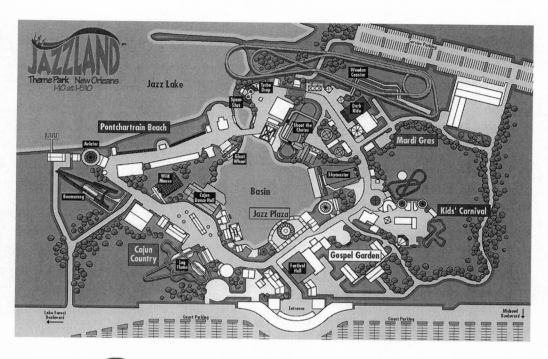

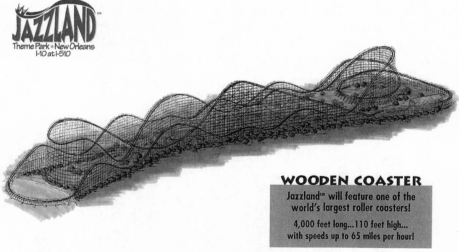

WOODEN COASTER

Jazzland℠ will feature one of the world's largest roller coasters!

4,000 feet long...110 feet high... with speeds up to 65 miles per hour!

Opening Spring 2000, Jazzland℠ Theme Park will feature spectacular rides, food and live entertainment on 140 acres just minutes from downtown New Orleans. Located at the intersection of I-10 and I-510, the park will be open daily during summer months; weekends during fall & spring.

www.jazzland2000.com

Top: Map (Jazzland). Bottom: Mega Zeph (Jazzland).

coaster has three inversions and two 125-foot towers, one at each end of the track. The train follows the circuit, climbs the second tower and is then released in reverse back to the station.

MEGA ZEPH (2000)   Designed by Custom Coasters International, this is a double out-and-back with 4,000 feet of wooden track laid on a steel structure. From a 110-foot-tall lift the first drop is straight forward at 65 mph leading into a series of hills associated with "airtime."

FAMILY COASTER (2000)   A tame roller coaster designed for parents and children.

Funtown USA
774 Portland Rd.
Saco, Maine 04072
www.funtownsplashtownusa.com

This 77-acre park opened in 1967 and is home to the only wooden roller coaster in the state of Maine.

EXCALIBUR (1998)   Designed by Custom Coasters International, this wooden twister/out-and-back has a 100-foot-tall lift with a 55-mph, 90-foot drop. The 2,700-foot-long track passes through itself five times, including a figure-eight, before heading back to the castle station.

GALIXI (1978)   Individual cars run along this compact steel coaster that is laid out as a four layer figure-eight.

Excalibur (Renee Buck).

Excalibur (Cory Cormier).

Excalibur

TECHNICAL FACTS ABOUT THE EXCALIBUR

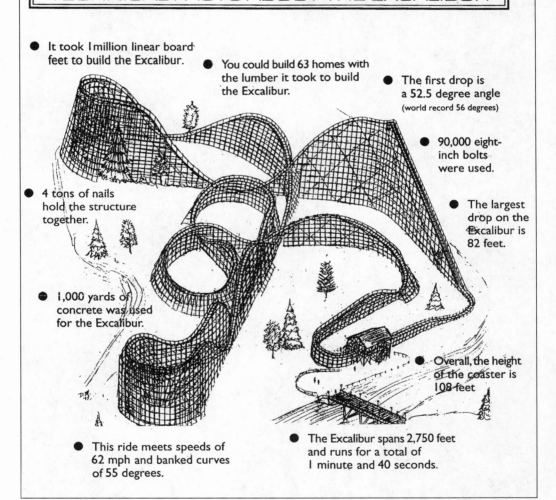

- It took 1 million linear board feet to build the Excalibur.

- You could build 63 homes with the lumber it took to build the Excalibur.

- The first drop is a 52.5 degree angle (world record 56 degrees)

- 90,000 eight-inch bolts were used.

- 4 tons of nails hold the structure together.

- The largest drop on the Excalibur is 82 feet.

- 1,000 yards of concrete was used for the Excalibur.

- Overall, the height of the coaster is 108 feet

- This ride meets speeds of 62 mph and banked curves of 55 degrees.

- The Excalibur spans 2,750 feet and runs for a total of 1 minute and 40 seconds.

Excalibur (Funtown, USA).

Six Flags America

P.O. Box 4210
Largo, Maryland 20775
www.sixflags.com

This park opened in 1982 as Wild World, then became Adventure World before re-opening in 1999 as Six Flags America.

WILD ONE (1917)   Formerly the Giant at Paragon Park, this coaster was moved to Wild World and made its debut in 1986. This 4,000-foot-long woodie was originally designed and built by John Miller and the Philadelphia Toboggan Company. The lift hill is 98-feet high and the track drops at a 52-degree angle to begin the 2 minute ride at 55 miles per hour. This coaster was once the longest and highest in New England and was well known in the Boston area for its history since it was a favorite of local and national celebrities. The Kennedys, Judy Garland, and Ted Williams all rode the coaster numerous times, and Boston's Cardinal Cushing celebrated his birthday on the giant coaster each year.

THE MIND ERASER (1995)   Vekoma designed this suspended coaster with multiple inversions, dangling riders legs and feet from a 100-foot lift to just 9-feet above ground.

ROAR (1998)   Called "the greatest wooden coaster on the face of the earth" by major league baseball star Cal Ripken, Jr., this wooden twister contains six reversals and twenty cross-overs. The 3,200-foot-long track designed by Great Coasters International has a first lift of 90 feet and a second drop that spirals 180 degrees resulting in a force of nearly 3.5 G's. Several instances of weightlessness occur at speeds up to 50 mph.

TWO FACE: THE FLIP SIDE (1999)   The perfect theme for this Vekoma boomerang. Face to face and suspended, this inverted steel coaster pulls riders up a 137-foot lift before releasing them at 55 miles per hour through 1,000 feet of track that includes the "boomerang" and a 72-foot-tall vertical loop. Then again, in reverse!

THE JOKER'S JINX (1999)   A set of 44 linear inductions motors create a traveling magnetic wave that pushes the train from a stationary standpoint to 60 mph in just over 3 seconds. In less than two minutes, 2,705 feet of track are traced through a compact, steel maze of twisting, turning and looping. Premier Rides designed this LIM coaster with 4 vertical loops, 30 vertical curves, 25 compound horizontal curves and 1 corkscrew.

Wild One (Wild World).

Top: Roar (Great Coasters International). Bottom: Two Face: The Flip Side (Six Flags America).

The Joker's Jinx (Six Flags America).

THE JOKER'S JINX

linear induction motor (LIM)
roller coaster blasts riders
from 0-60 mph in just over 3 seconds.
The high-speed blast off
sends passengers through a 500-ton
steel maze featuring 30 vertical curves,
25 horizontal curves
and four complete inversions.

Manufactured by Premier Rides, Inc.
401 Headquarters Dr. Suite 201, Millersville, MD (410) 923-0414

13710 Central Avenue
Largo, MD 20721
(301) 249-1500

SixFlags®
AMERICA

BATMAN and all related characters, names, rides and
attractions and indicia are trademarks of DC Comics © 1999

The Joker's Jinx (Six Flags America).

Six Flags New England
Box 307
Agawam, Massachusetts 01001
www.sixflags.com

This is a traditional amusement park that got its start in 1840 as a picnic grove called "Gallups Grove." In the late 1880s, the name was changed to "Riverside Grove" before being shortened to just "Riverside" in 1912. At this time Riverside Amusement Park began to evolve into New England's largest. Today the park is part of Premier Park's Six Flags family.

RIVERSIDE CYCLONE (1983)   Designed by William Cobb, this coaster has been called the most bone-jarring, harrowing ride in America. Although it does not set any records, the 3,600 feet of track represent sheer terror. It is built in a small area, requiring steeper drops and quicker turns. The lift hill has a 28-degree slope and the first drop takes the train from 0 to 60 miles per hour in just 3 seconds down a 54-degree banked twisting fall into a 60-degree high-speed bank turn.

Riverside Cyclone (Six Flags New England).

BLACK WIDOW (1977)   On this Arrow Dynamics–designed steel shuttle loop, the train launches forward down a 50-foot drop at 45 miles per hour into a 360-degree loop before stopping at a second "launchpad." The trip is then repeated — backwards!

THUNDERBOLT (1940)   Originally named the Cyclone, the coaster was designed from original blueprints used to build the coaster for the 1939 New York World's Fair. This wooden classic is 70 feet high, 2,865 feet long, and runs for 60 seconds.

MIND ERASER (1996)   This steel inverted coaster was designed by Vekoma. The 2,172 feet of track includes a 115-foot lift hill and 5 elements that suspend riders upside-down at speeds up to 64 mph.

ROLLING THUNDER (1996)   A Miler designed junior steel roller coaster for a tamer experience.

Whalom Park

Route 13
Fitchburg, Massachusetts 01420
www.whalom.com

Thunderbolt (John Atashian).

Whalom Park is a traditional amusement park, located about 45 miles west of Boston. Since 1893, the people of New England have attended this park for the beaches, boating and picnic facilities. It is also home to a classic Philadelphia Toboggan Company coaster.

FLYER COMET (1940)   This is a classic wooden figure-eight, designed by the Philadelphia Toboggan Company. With a 70-foot-tall lift hill, the train can achieve a maximum speed of 35 miles per hour. Although the ride is not of great length, it represents a terrific link to the past.

Flyer Comet (Whalom Park).

Michigan's Adventure
4750 Whitehall Road
Muskegon, Michigan 49445
www.miadventure.com

Opening in 1968, this is Michigan's largest amusement park and is home of the only wooden roller coaster in the state.

CORKSCREW (1979)   This is one of Arrow Dynamics' basic corkscrew designs: 70 feet high, 1,250 feet long, and a top speed of 45 miles per hour.

Corkscrew (Michigan's Adventure).

WOLVERINE WILDCAT (1988)   A 3,000-foot-long natural colored wooden double-out-and-back designed and built by Curtis D. Summers and Charles Dinn. This 2 minute ride begins from an 85-foot-high lift and reaches a top speed of 55 miles per hour.

ZACH'S ZOOMER (1994)   A junior size wooden coaster with 2,000 feet of track designed by Custom Coasters International.

SHIVERING TIMBERS (1998)   This massive wooden out-and-back was designed by Custom Coasters International and has 5,384 feet of undulating track. With an initial lift hill of 125 feet, the train drops 120 feet at 65 mph and then climbs to drop 100 feet followed by yet another drop of 95 feet. The grand finale of this 2½ minute coaster ride is a double helix.

MAD MOUSE (1999)   These individual cars climb 68 feet to begin a wild ride full of hairpin turns. Patterned after the classic, the track is 1,268 feet long and was designed by Arrow Dynamics.

Wolverine Wildcat (Michigan's Adventure).

BIG DIPPER (1999)　A steel junior coaster built by Chance and designed for a family experience.

Knott's Camp Snoopy
Mall of America
5000 Center Court
Bloomington, Minnesota 55425-5500
www.campsnoopy.com

Operation of this indoor amusement park began in 1992 as part of the nation's largest shopping center, Mall of America. The park was created by Knott's Berry Farm as the centerpiece to Bloomington's mega-mall, which was developed by the builders of the West Edmonton Mall in Canada.

PEPSI RIPSAW ROLLER COASTER (1992)　This coaster was designed by Zierer to be a milder family type of ride, electrically driven through 2,680 feet of track. The entire ride lasts 2½ minutes and reaches a top speed of 27 mph at a maximum height of 60 feet above the ground — all within the Mall of America's seven acre center courtyard.

LI'L SHAVER (1995)　A 150-foot-long steel Zamperla children's coaster.

Valleyfair

One Valleyfair Drive
Shakopee, Minnesota 55379
www.valleyfair.com

Bordering the Minnesota River, this 90-acre park opened in 1976. Today it is owned and operated by Cedar Fair L.P.

HIGH ROLLER (1976) Designed by International Amusement Devices, Inc. of Dayton, Ohio, this is a 2,982-foot-long wooden out-and-back L-shaped course. It has a 70-foot-high lift and a ride time of 1 minute, 45 seconds with a top speed of 50 miles per hour.

High Roller (Valleyfair).

WILDRAILS (1979) Created by Anton Schwarzkopf of Germany, Wildrails features a 50-foot-high steel figure-eight with spirals. Individual cars, which seat four, reach speeds of 40–50 miles per hour along a 1,054-foot-long track. The entire ride lasts 1 minute, 34 seconds.

CORKSCREW (1980)   Created by Arrow Dynamics, this is a steel double corkscrew coaster that is 85 feet high and 1,950 feet long.

EXCALIBUR (1989)   A wooden structure with tubular steel track designed by Arrow Dynamics, Excalibur is 105 feet high with a 60-degree first drop and has eight track crisscrosses along the 2,415-foot-long course. The ride lasts 2 minutes, 17 seconds and reaches a top speed of 55 miles per hour.

Excalibur (Valleyfair).

WILD THING (1996) Morgan Manufacturing designed this steel "hyper coaster" at a cost of $10 million. The 3-minute ride begins with a 207-foot lift and drops 200 feet at 74 mph following the 5,460-foot-long out-and-back course.

Wild Thing (Dan Feicht).

MAD MOUSE (1999)   Reminiscent of the old carnival coaster, this family-oriented ride is 50 feet high and features a combination of sudden dips, serpentine curves and hairpin turns. Individual "mouse" cars reach speeds of 30 mph as they follow 1,257 feet of track.

MILD THING KIDDIE COASTER (1976)   This steel junior coaster is one of Allen Herschell's designs.

Mad Mouse (Valleyfair).

Silver Dollar City

HC 1, Box 791
Branson, Missouri 65616
www.silverdollarcity.com

"You have a great past ahead of you" sums up the historical charm of this crafts showplace. In 1949, the Herschend family signed a 99-year lease for Marvel Cave, and in 1960 opened the fictitious 1890s Ozark mountain community based on legend.

THUNDERATION (1993)   Designed by Arrow Dynamics, this 3,022-foot-long coaster is a runaway mine train type that begins with an 81-foot high lift and runs for 2 minutes, 10 seconds at 55 mph. Covering six acres, it includes 60-degree banked turns and a 79-degree double helix.

FIRE IN THE HOLE (1978)   For around 3 minutes, this in-house designed modern day scenic railway winds its way through a town set ablaze by the local Baldknobbers. Completely enclosed, this ride has a 1,520-foot-long track and only travels at 8 feet per second, with the exception of the 30 mph strategic drops (one in which you will get wet).

BUZZSAW FALLS (1999)   Premier Rides and Silver Dollar City designed this "liquid coaster" as the world's first water flume ride and high-speed roller coaster in one. The 3 minute, 2,263-foot-long journey begins as a boat ride before it threads on rails for the 50 mph coaster portion, climaxing with a 118-foot plunge into a free-floating finale.

Thunderation (Silver Dollar City).

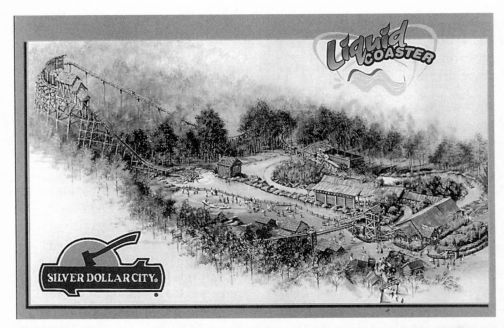

Top and Bottom: Buzzsaw Falls (Premier Rides, Inc.).

Buzzsaw Falls (Premier Rides, Inc.).

Worlds of Fun
4545 Worlds of Fun Avenue
Kansas City, Missouri 64161
www.worldsof fun.com

In 1973 this park opened with a theme of "Around the World in Eighty Days." Today it is operated by Cedar Fair L.P.

ORIENT EXPRESS (1980)   A steel coaster that features interlocking loops and a Kamikaze Kurve (the world's first boomerang), a ride innovation that turns passengers upside down in each of two barrel rolls within 13 seconds. The ride is 3,470 feet long with a first drop of 115 feet at a 55-degree angle. It has five drops in all, and a top speed of 65 miles per hour. In addition, this Arrow Dynamics design, which lasts 2 minutes, 30 seconds, has a 100-foot-long tunnel. The ride reaches a reported G-force of 3.5.

Orient Express (Worlds of Fun).

TIMBER WOLF (1989)   Designed by Curtis D. Summers, this wooden coaster is ten stories tall with a 95-foot drop. It speeds along the 4,230-foot-long track with hairpin turns and an unusual 560-degree helix at 53 miles per hour. The ride lasts for about 2½ minutes.

Timber Wolf (Worlds of Fun).

MAMBA (1998)   This steel structure has a first hill of 205 feet and a second hill of 184 feet. It is a 5,600-foot-long "hyper" coaster by D.H. Morgan that reaches speeds of 75 miles per hour during its 3 minute out-and-back run.

WACKY WORM (1993)   For the beginner, this is a junior steel coaster only 444 feet long designed by Pinfari.

Mamba (Worlds of Fun).

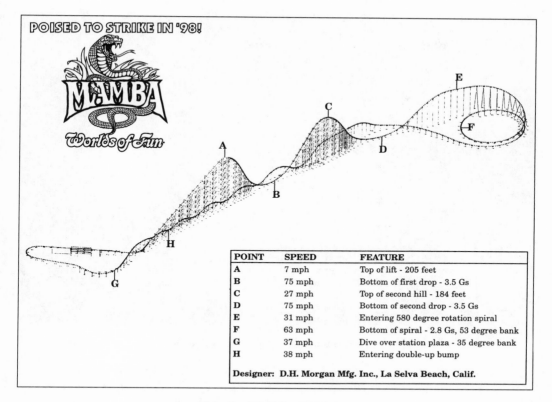

Mamba (Worlds of Fun).

Six Flags St. Louis

P.O. Box 60
Eureka, Missouri 63025
www.sixflags.com

Opened in 1971 as Six Flags Over Mid-America, today it is one of many owned and operated by Premier Parks.

THE SCREAMIN' EAGLE (1976)   It was built as the world's longest, tallest, and fastest. It is 110 feet high, 3,872 feet long, and originally had a top speed of 62 miles per hour. Designed by John Allen and engineered by Bill Cobb, the ride features a unique "swoop curve" that slows the cars momentarily before plunging them down the track's first 87-foot precipice and into their 62 miles per hour ride only to climb to the ride's highest point for a second dive 92 feet straight down.

In 1990, new faster cars replaced the older ones and increased the speeds from 62 miles per hour to 70 miles per hour. The major contribution to the increased speed comes from the fact that each car, with the exception

The Screamin' Eagle (Six Flags St. Louis).

of the lead car, has only two sets of wheels versus four, thereby creating less friction and less resistance on the track. Quick acceleration and a sense of weightlessness is caused by the space tolerance allowed between the top and bottom wheels. With the absence of the second set of wheels, the floating sensation that riders experience when careening down the Screamin' Eagle's steep hills is now intensified.

NINJA (1989)   This is a steel coaster designed by Vekoma Ride Manufacturing that takes riders upside down four times. At 2,430 feet long and 110 feet high, the ride has a top speed of 65 miles per hour. This coaster was originally located in Vancouver, Canada, as part of the World's Fair in 1986 before being dismantled and moved to Six Flags.

RIVER KING MINE TRAIN (1971)   Another mine train type of coaster installed during the early Seventies and designed by Arrow Dynamics. This was the original coaster of Six Flags (actually there were two, but one was sold to Dollywood).

BATMAN: THE RIDE (1995)   Designed by Bolliger & Mabillard, this is the world's fourth inverted, looping thrill ride themed to Batman. Featuring five head-over-heels experiences, the 2,693-foot-long coaster begins with a 105-foot lift and reaches 50 mph during the 2-minute adventure.

MR. FREEZE (1997)   Using Premier Rides' linear induction motors, this 1,382-foot-long coaster reaches 70 mph and 4 G's within 4 seconds. Shot

Ninja (Six Flags St. Louis).

from a 190-foot tunnel and into a vertical climb while twisting to enter a 180-degree inversion, this ride's halfway point is at 226 feet above the ground where the entire trip repeats in reverse.

ACME GRAVITY POWERED ROLLER RIDE (1975)   This is a themed, 200-foot-long children's coaster by Chance.

THE BOSS (2000)   From a 120 foot tall lift this 5000 foot long wooden terrain twister begins with a 100 foot 52-degree drop, flattens out, turns left and dives an additional 50 feet into a natural ravine. Designed by Custom Coasters International, this 60 MPH woodie includes three more ravine drops, several swoop turns, a large double dip and a 565-degree helix finale.

Mr. Freeze (Six Flags St. Louis).

Adventuredome

Circus Circus
2880 Las Vegas Boulevard South
Las Vegas, Nevada 89109-1120
www.adventuredome.com

Within a gigantic pink glass dome is one of the largest enclosed amusement parks in the United States. Opening in 1993, this 5-acre park initiated the new Vegas image of a "family" destination.

CANYON BLASTER (1993) The 2,423-foot-long double-looping corkscrew layout was designed by Arrow Dynamics. It has a first drop of 66 feet from a lift of 94 feet and a top speed of 55 miles per hour during the 1 minute, 45 second ride.

Adventuredome (Circus Circus).

Canyon Blaster (Circus Circus).

New York-New York Hotel & Casino
3790 South Las Vegas Blvd.
Las Vegas, Nevada 89109
www.nynyhotelcasino.com

Together, Primadonna Resorts and MGM Grand developed and opened this property in 1997. The tallest hotel towers in Nevada are one-third scale replicas of the actual New York architecture. Among the many extensively themed areas within this hotel is Coney Island.

MANHATTAN EXPRESS (1997)   From inside the casino the taxi cab themed train begins the 203-foot lift ascent through the roof. The initial drop of 75 feet is just a warm-up for the 144-foot second drop at 67 mph on this 4,777-foot-long track. From the third hill riders encounter a dizzying succession of high banked turns, camel back hills, a vertical loop, a 540-degree spiral, and finally, a heartland twist and dive. Designed by Togo, this four minute experience is similar to an actual cab ride in New York!

New York-New York (**Global Architectural Models**).

Sahara

2535 South Las Vegas Blvd.
Las Vegas, Nevada 89109
www.pcap.com/sahara.htm

Opening in 1952, the Sahara is one of the original hotels on the famous Las Vegas strip. After major renovations, this resort now offers an area dedicated to auto racing which includes the NASCAR Cafe, race car simulators, a gift store and a roller coaster.

SPEED: THE RIDE (2000) Designed by Premier Rides, this steel coaster uses linear induction motors to launch the train from 0 to 60+ mph within four seconds. The track leaves the building, turns south, dives into a 100-foot long tunnel and emerges into a 74-foot-tall loop followed by a squeeze between the Sahara sign's pylons. At this point, the coaster climbs a 244-foot-tall tower...hesitates...and drops backwards, following the track in reverse.

Premier Rides
401 Headquarters Drive
Suite 201-202

Sahara Coaster (Premier Rides, Inc.).

Stratosphere

2000 South Las Vegas Blvd.
Las Vegas, Nevada 89104
www.klas-tv.com/stratosphere/

In 1996, after four years of construction, the $550 million Stratosphere Resort opened as the tallest building west of the Mississippi. The top of the 1,149-foot-tall tower offers a roller coaster, an observation deck, a revolving restaurant and the Big Shot which propels the adventurous another 160 feet skyward before freefalling back.

HIGH ROLLER (1996)   More than 100 stories above ground, the world's highest roller coaster wraps around the tower's top. Just above the observation deck, this 30 mph ride navigates 865 feet of tame track offering the greatest panoramic view of all time — if you can keep your eyes open!

Buffalo Bill's

I-15 South Stateline
Primm, Nevada 89193-5997
www.primadonna.com

One of three hotel/casinos located at the California-Nevada border on I-15. This entire resort area was developed by the Primm family and is now a wholly owned subsidiary of MGM Grand.

THE DESPERADO (1994)   At a lift height of 209 feet, this Arrow Dynamics designed steel coaster beat out Magnum XL-200 by 4 feet for the honor

Above: High Roller (Stratosphere). Following page: Stratosphere (Stratosphere).

of the world's tallest when it opened. The 5,900-foot-long, 3 minute experience begins with a lift through the casino roof and a first drop of 225 feet at 80 mph into a tunnel in the desert floor.

MAXFLIGHT **VR2002**   OK…this is not a "real" coaster, but it's worth a mention. It is described as the world's first customer programmable, virtual reality, full motion cyber coaster that allows you to control the experience. Secured in the two-seat pod, the individually tailored rides are capable of 360-degree loops, spins and spiral action while viewing the 58-inch monitors. For special effects, you will feel the wind and hear the rumble of the track.

Canobie Lake Park
P.O. Box 190
Salem, New Hampshire 03079
www.canobie.com

This traditional park opened in 1902 as a street car (trolley) amusement facility and today still has several of the original buildings.

The Desperado (Buffalo Bill's).

THE YANKEE CANNONBALL (1930)　This coaster was originally built by the Philadelphia Toboggan Company for Lakewood Park in Waterbury, Connecticut. In 1936, it was purchased by Canobie Lake Park and moved. This wooden out-and-back is about 2,000 feet long and has a first drop of 63½ feet. With a top speed of 35 miles per hour, the ride lasts a little less than 2 minutes. In 1954, Hurricane Carol demolished the first hill, but it was repaired. In 1976, a fire destroyed the station, yet this classic coaster, which the late John Allen proclaimed as the smoothest riding of his day, continues to roll on.

CANOBIE CORKSCREW (1975)　Originally operated in Old Chicago and the Alabama State Fair before being moved here in 1990, it was designed by Arrow Dynamics.

The Yankee Cannonball (Canobie Lake Park).

Canobie Corkscrew (Canobie Lake Park).

Clementon Amusement Park
Box 125
Clementon, New Jersey 08021

Clementon remains as the last of the great turn-of-the-century amusement parks in the Philadelphia area. It has been owned and operated by the same family since its beginning in 1907.

> JACK RABBIT (1919)   Designed by John Miller, this is the second oldest Philadelphia Toboggan coaster still operating. The wooden figure-eight is 1,380 feet in length with a lift of 50 feet. It is basically a side-friction coaster with no under-wheels.

Six Flags Great Adventure
P.O. Box 120
Jackson, New Jersey 08527
www.sixflags.com

Called America's largest seasonal theme park, this facility also includes a 4½ mile drive-through safari full of wild animals. Opened in 1974 this park became part of the Six Flags chain when it was purchased by Ballys in 1982.

RUNAWAY TRAIN (1973)   One of Arrow Dynamics' mine train coasters, the tubular steel track provides for a smooth family-type ride.

ROLLING THUNDER (1979)   Designed by Don Rosser and engineered by William Cobb, this wooden twin-track out-and-back is 3,200 feet long and has a lift hill of 96 feet. Its top speed of 56 miles per hour occurs as the train reaches the bottom of the first drop.

GREAT AMERICAN SCREAM MACHINE (1989)   Arrow Dynamics designed this steel coaster with seven inversions: three vertical loops, a double corkscrew, and a boomerang. The track is 3,800 feet long and has a lift height of 173 feet. The train can reach 68 miles per hour during its 155-foot first drop on a ride lasting 2 minutes, 20 seconds.

BATMAN: THE RIDE (1993)   This is a Bolliger & Mabillard inverted coaster 2,693 feet in length with five inversions including two vertical outside loops, two outside helices, and a zero-gravity roll. The 2 minute, 50 miles per hour ride starts from a 105-foot-high lift.

BATMAN & ROBIN: THE CHILLER (1998)   Not one, but two LIM coasters by Premier Rides. Robin, (the red track) is 1,229 feet long, and Batman (the blue track) is 1,137 feet long. Both hit speeds of 70 mph within seconds and both climb to a height of 200 feet after following similar but slightly different courses. The entire ride, forward and backward, is approximately 45 seconds.

MEDUSA (1999)   Bolliger & Mabillard designed this 3,985-foot-long steel coaster as the first of its kind—floorless! The train is without body, essentially leaving the rider perched upon a pedestal over the track for 3 minutes and 15 seconds. The lift is 142 feet tall which drops at 61 mph through 7 inversions.

VIPER (1995)   This steel coaster covered in rings was designed by Togo International. Known for the "heartline roll," this coaster is 1,670 feet long, 88.6 feet tall and has a top speed of 48 mph.

Rolling Thunder (Six Flags Great Adventure).

Great American Scream Machine (Six Flags Great Adventure).

SKULL MOUNTAIN (1996)   This enclosed design by Intamin covers 1,377 feet within 1 minute, 40 seconds at a top speed of 33 mph.

Morey's Pier
3501 Boardwalk
Wildwood, New Jersey 08260
www.moreyspiers.com

Family owned and operated, the Morey brothers opened Morey's Surf Side Pier at 25th Street & Boardwalk in 1969 with one giant slide. This site has expanded over time and with the acquisitions of the 1931 Marine Pier at Schellenger and the pier at Spencer, Morey's Piers now includes three amusement park locations along the boardwalk.

SEA SERPENT (1984)   A Vekoma designed boomerang with 875 feet of track anchored at each end with a 125-foot-tall tower. The first drop is 115 feet at 45 mph leading into three inversions that will be traveled forward and backward.

FLITZER (1983)   This is a 500-foot-long steel European carnival coaster designed by Anton Schwarzkopf.

Batman : The Ride (Six Flags Great Adventure).

DUELING LINEAR INDUCTION SHUTTLE LOOP COASTER

This page and following page: Batman and Robin: The Chiller (Premier Rides, Inc.).

JET STAR (1970)   Relocated here in 1993, this Schwarzkopf coaster has 1,766 feet of steel track within a compact figure-eight layout.

THE GREAT NOR'EASTER (1995)   With your legs dangling below, this suspended steel coaster cruises through five inversions along 2,100 feet of track at speeds up to 55 mph. The $5 million investment designed by Vekoma also includes a lift hill of 115 feet and a first drop of 95 feet.

THE GREAT WHITE (1996)   Custom Coasters International designed this out-and-back with a steel frame and a 3,300-foot-long wooden layered track. This entire coaster that was built on 600 pilings over the beach begins with a 50 mph first drop of 100 feet and ends with a dive under the boardwalk.

DOO WOPPER (1998)   This drive-in themed wild mouse ride includes sudden hairpin turns and sharp drops.

ROLLIE'S COASTER (1999)   Designed for family enjoyment, this steel coaster is a classic 40-foot-high figure-eight.

Astroland
1000 Surf Avenue
Coney Island, New York 11224
www.astroland.com

The world-famous Cyclone has been a part of this park since 1975. In July 1977, *Town and Country* magazine called this classic the perfect roller coaster: "It never stops or slows for a second after it leaves the lift. Its drops, turns, and twists are unsurpassed in the coaster world and it is as smooth and graceful as a seagull. New Yorkers should consider the Cyclone as valuable as the Statue of Liberty or the Empire State Building."

CYCLONE (1927)   Designed by Vernon Keenan and built by Harry C. Baker, this coaster required an initial investment of $175,000. The lift hill is 85 feet high and drops at a 60-degree angle, which pushes the train to 60 miles per hour. The 3,000-foot-long track also includes six fan turns and nine drops. The entire ride lasts for 1 minute, 50 seconds. Charles Lindbergh once said that the thrill of the Cyclone even beat the thrill of flying.

Deno's Wonder Wheel Amusement Park
Boardwalk at West 12th Street
Coney Island, New York 11224
www.wonderwheel.com

Cyclone (Astroland).

Established in 1981, the centerpiece of this boardwalk amusement park is the world famous 1920 Wonder Wheel, which is sort of a cross between a ferris wheel and a roller coaster.

SEA SERPENT (1999)   Custom designed for Deno's, this steel roller coaster is tailored for the entire family with great views of the boardwalk and the beach.

Six Flags Darien Lake
9993 Allegheny Road
P.O. Box 91
Darien Center, New York 14040-0091
www.sixflags.com

Beginning as a campground in 1964, this facility has evolved into New York's coaster capital. The waterslides were added in 1977 and the first coaster arrived in 1982. Premier Parks, Inc., became the park's parent company in 1995 which led to the Six Flags brand in 1998.

Cyclone (Astroland).

PREDATOR (1990)   Designed by Curtis D. Summers, this is New York's largest wooden roller coaster. The 2 minute ride is laid out in an L-shape that crosses through itself, with a lot of action on the curves. This ride has very few straight sections and a total of twelve drops. It is 3,400 feet long and 99 feet high.

THE VIPER (1982)   This is a steel coaster by Arrow Dynamics that has a series of five upside-down turns. Down a 75-foot drop within 4 seconds, the train reaches 50 miles per hour and enters the vertical loop followed by a double corkscrew and a boomerang curve.

SUPERMAN RIDE OF STEEL (1999)   Representing the single largest attraction investment to date, the $12 million steel "hyper" coaster is over one mile long at 5,350 feet. Designed by Intamin, the first drop is 205 feet from an initial lift of 208 feet, giving the 3 minute ride a top speed of 75 mph.

BOOMERANG COAST TO COASTER (1998)   One of Vekoma's triple looping steel coasters. With a backwards lift of 125 feet, the train is released to follow the 938-foot course before pausing upon another lift. Then returning along the same route in reverse back to the station, all of this in 90 seconds.

MIND ERASER (1997)   This inverted suspended-looping coaster is 100

Predator (Six Flags Darien Lake).

Top: Predator (Six Flags Darien Lake). Bottom: The Viper (Six Flags Darien Lake).

Top: Superman Ride of Steel. Bottom: Mind Eraser (Six Flags Darien Lake).

feet tall, 2,172 feet long and runs for 2 minutes. Designed by Vekoma International, riders on this coaster are suspended from the track, with legs and feet dangling as the speed reaches 60 mph at times.

Martin's Fantasy Island

2400 Grand Island Blvd.
Grand Island, New York 14072
www.martinsfantasyisland.com

Located on an island just down stream from Niagara Falls, this 80-acre park opened in 1994 with several themed areas.

SILVER COMET (1999)   An out-and-back with elements of a twister, structured in galvanized steel and layered with a wood track. The two minute ride begins with a lift of 95 feet and a 90-foot first drop at 60 mph. Custom Coasters International designed this 3,000-foot-long roller coaster.

WILDCAT (1975)   Relocated here, this 50-foot-high steel figure-eight was designed by Anton Schwarzkopf. Individual cars traverse the 1,800 feet of track within a minute and a half.

Silver Comet (Martin's Fantasy Island).

The Great Escape

P.O. Box 511
Lake George, New York 12845
www.thegreatescape.com

This traditional amusement park opened in 1954 and is now owned and operated by Premier Parks.

STEAMIN' DEMON (1978)   This is the second classic steel track corkscrew with a loop designed by Arrow Dynamics. Relocated here in 1984 from Pontchartrain Beach in New Orleans where it was known as "Ragin' Cajun."

BOOMERANG COAST TO COASTER (1997)   One of Vekoma's forward-backward coasters covering 875 feet of track and 3 inversions each way.

THE NIGHTMARE (1999)   Housed in a six story building, this Schwarzkopf coaster is 45 feet tall and has 1,772 feet of track. Individual cars seating four race through the darkness at 34 mph.

THE COMET (1947)   Consistently ranked as one of the top roller coasters by enthusiasts, this classic has the distinction of being the only wooden coaster to be built three times. When the infamous Crystal Beach Cyclone

Steamin' Demon (The Great Escape).

THE GREAT ESCAPE.
SPLASHWATER KINGDOM

New for 1999-- The Nightmare Roller Coaster brings suspense, surprises and sensations unlike anything ever experienced before on a Great Escape coaster. This enclosed ride races in complete darkness through a monstrous, six-story, 16,000 square foot mysterious cave. Riders soar, plunge, twist and turn, sitting in individual trains that, at times, pass near each other.

The Nightmare (The Great Escape).

(1927) was dismantled in 1946, the structural steel was salvaged and incorporated into the New Comet to support the nine layer, 4,197-foot-long wooden track. This double out-and-back was designed by Herbert Schmeck of the Philadelphia Toboggan Company and ran until the closing of Crystal Beach in 1989. Purchased at auction for $210,000, the Comet was rebuilt and opened once more in 1994 thanks to Charles R. Wood.

Seabreeze
4600 Culver Road
Rochester, New York 14622-1399
www.seabreeze.com

Over the long history of this park, which opened in 1879, there have been six coasters located here: the Figure-Eight (1903), the Greyhound (1918), the Jack Rabbit (1920), the Virginia Reel (1921), the Wildcat (1922), and the Bobsleds (1968). Two of these remain today. Owned by the Long family (associated with carousels) since

THE GREAT ESCAPE.
SPLASHWATER KINGDOM

The #1 rated Comet Roller Coaster zooms over 4,197 feet of wooden track -- the length of three football fields-- and boasts 14 climbs and drops. The highest climb is 95 feet, then it drops its passengers almost straight down at a 50-degree angle.

The Comet (The Great Excape).

the 1940s, this park was renamed "Dreamland" until the 1970s, when the original name was reinstated.

JACK RABBIT (1920)   This is a wooden modified figure-eight designed by the Philadelphia Toboggan Company. The first lift is 75 feet high and the track is 2,130 feet long with a 265-foot-long tunnel along the way. At 42 mph maximum, the entire ride lasts 1 minute and 45 seconds.

Jack Rabbit (Seabreeze).

BOBSLEDS (1968)   Designed by George W. Long, this 1,240-foot-long coaster is constructed of wood with tubular steel track. Described as a triple decker figure-eight, the highest drop is only 28 feet and the top speed is 23 mph.

QUANTUM LOOP (1983)   Designed by E. Soquet SA, this double looper was relocated here in 1994. From 75 feet, the first drop is 72 feet at 56 mph. The length of the track is 2,822 feet and the ride time is 2 minutes.

BUNNY RABBIT (1960)   In 1985 this Herschel 100-foot-long kiddie coaster found a home at Seabreeze. The 2 minute ride only goes 10 mph.

BEAR TRAX (1997)   This is a 375-foot-long children's steel coaster designed by Fred Miler.

Bobsleds (Seabreeze).

Top: Quantum Loop (Seabreeze). Bottom: Bear Trax (Paul L. Ruben Archives).

Playland
Playland Parkway
Rye, New York 10580

Opening in 1928, Playland was America's first totally planned amusement park and the prototype for today's theme parks. It was completely and carefully planned as a family park by the Westchester Country Park Commission. Today, it has its place on the National Register of Historic Places and is managed by the Department of Parks, Recreation and Conservation.

From 1928 to 1957, this was the home of the famous Aeroplane Coaster designed by Fred Church. This 3,600-foot-long coaster was named in honor of Lindbergh's flight in 1927 and was similar to the Bobs-style coaster at Chicago's Riverview Park. It has been called the "greatest body wringer and most violent ride ever built."

DRAGON COASTER (1929)   Another wooden thriller designed by Fred Church, it is 80 feet high and 3,400 feet long. This 2 minute ride gives the impression of being hurled into the mouth of a dragon.

KIDDIE COASTER (1928)   This tame wooden ride was built by the National Amusement Device Company.

HURRICANE (1995)   Premier designed this 1,340-foot-long steel windstorm coaster.

Paramount's Carowinds
P.O. Box 410289
Charlotte, North Carolina 28241
www.carowinds.com

Located on the state line between North and South Carolina, Carowinds first opened in 1973. This park offers a unique atmosphere that is rich in Carolina heritage and full of Southern hospitality on both sides of the border.

THUNDER ROAD (1976)   This is a wooden twin-racing coaster that is 3,819 feet long and has a lift hill of 93 feet. Designed by John Allen, the ride takes 2 minutes, 10 seconds to complete, reaching a top speed of 58 miles per hour while averaging 42 mph.

CAROLINA CYCLONE (1980)   This is an Arrow Dynamics–designed steel quadruple-looping roller coaster. There are two consecutive 360-degree vertical loops followed by two consecutive 360-degree barrel rolls (corkscrew), and a 450-degree uphill helix.

GOLDRUSHER (1973)   The original coaster of the park designed by Arrow as a runaway mine train type.

Thunder Road (Paramount's Carowinds).

Top: Thunder Road. Bottom: Carolina Cyclone (Paramount's Carowinds).

Goldrusher (Paramount's Carowinds).

VORTEX (1992)   Designed by Bolliger & Mabillard of Switzerland, this coaster is a one-of-a-kind found only at Carowinds. Although there are other "stand-up" steel coasters, this is the first to provide an oblique loop as well as a vertical loop and a "flat-spin." Statistically, the track is 2,040 feet long with a 90-foot-tall lift that pushes the train to a top speed of 50 miles per hour. Each train holds 24 passengers, with every coach holding four people standing side by side. This shorter train (three cars) reduces the different experiences of riding in the front and the back. All of these elements make the Vortex a unique ride for which designer Claude Mabillard declared "the best coaster Bolliger & Mabillard has built up to now" in 1992.

THE HURLER (1994)   Designed by International Coaster, Inc., this 3,157-foot-long woodie is themed for the "Wayne's World" section. From an 83-foot lift the train can reach a top speed of 50 miles per hour during its "most-excellent" 2 minute run.

SCOOBY-DOO'S GHOSTER COASTER (1975)   A 1,356-foot-long wooden junior coaster designed by the Philadelphia Toboggan Company.

TAXI JAM (1998)   A small steel coaster designed especially for children by Miler Coaster Company. The 416-foot track has 2 turns and one spiral.

TOP GUN: THE JET COASTER (1999)   Bolliger & Mabillard's inverted steel coaster in which riders are suspended below the track with legs dangling. Among the six inversions encountered during this two and a half minute ride is the "flatspin," which is a corkscrew maneuver that turns riders 360 degrees in one smooth motion. The track length is 2,956 feet and the height of the lift is 113 feet, which initiates the 62 mph ride.

Vortex (Paramount's Carowinds).

The Hurler (Paramount's Carowinds).

Scooby-Doo's Ghoster Coaster (Paramount's Carowinds).

Top Gun: The Jet Coaster (Paramount's Carowinds).

Top Gun: The Jet Coaster (Paramount's Carowinds).

Ghost Town in the Sky
US Highway 19
Maggie Valley, North Carolina 28751
www.ghosttowninthesky.com

Located on top of a mountain near the Smoky Mountains, this 275-acre park opened in 1961. To gain entry you have the option of a 3,364-foot-long incline railway, the adjacent two-seat chairlift, or a van service.

RED DEVIL (1988)   One of the first coasters designed by O.D. Hopkins Association, Inc., it is a single-looping, 2,037-foot-long ride with a top speed of 50 miles per hour. The unusual part of this coaster is that the 90-foot-high lift is not reached until the end of the 2 minute run.

Red Devil (Ghost Town in the Sky).

Six Flags Ohio
1060 North Aurora Road
Aurora, Ohio 44202
www.geaugalake.com

This traditional lake park has a rich history dating back to 1888. In 1995, Premier Parks, Inc., took over the ownership and operation.

THE RAGING WOLF BOBS (1988)   A wooden coaster inspired by the infamous wooden Riverview Bobs at Riverview Park in Chicago, Illinois (1924–1967). Designed by the Dinn Corporation, this coaster is 80 feet high and over a half a mile long. Speeds reach 50 miles per hour and some curves are banked up to 55-degrees. Riding time is approximately 2 minutes.

THE BIG DIPPER (1926)   This old wooden coaster, designed by John Miller, was completely over-hauled in 1980. It is 65 feet high, 2,680 feet long, and has a top speed of only 32 miles per hour. The total ride time is 1 minute, 45 seconds.

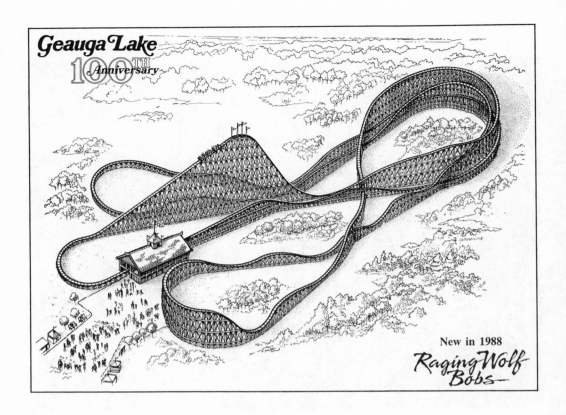

New in 1988

Raging Wolf Bobs

Top: The Raging Wolf Bobs. Bottom: The Big Dipper (Geauga Lake).

The Big Dipper (Geauga Lake).

Double Loop (Geauga Lake).

The Mind Eraser (Geauga Lake).

Serial Thriller (Geauga Lake).

DOUBLE LOOP (1977)   Designed by Arrow Dynamics, this was America's first vertical double-looping coaster. This steel coaster is 95 feet high, 1,800 feet long, and has a top speed of 36 miles per hour.

THE MIND ERASER (1996)   Forwards and backwards through the boomerang and vertical loop from 125-foot-tall lift towers. Designed by Vekoma, this 875-foot long coaster is like experiencing déjà vu … again!

SERIAL THRILLER (1998)   As your feet dangle below, the train slowly ascends the 120-foot hill, beginning a 50 mph, minute and a half ride that will take you through seven inversions. This is a $10 million coaster with 2,037 feet of steel track.

Paramount's Kings Island
P.O. Box 901
Kings Island, Ohio 45034
www.pki.com

This park opened in 1972 after the century-old Coney Island amusement park, which was located on the banks of the Ohio River in Cincinnati, closed because of constant flooding. Most of the attractions, including the ginkgo trees lining the Coney Mall, were transplanted from the old park to this section of Kings Island.

Coney Island Amusement Park (1954 view of Coney Island).

Top: The Beast. Bottom: Vortex (Paramount's Kings Island).

The Beast (Paramount's Kings Island).

THE BEAST (1979)   It took three years to design and construct this wooden coaster, which is the world's longest at 7,400 feet. Built on 35 densely wooded acres, the riding time is 4 minutes, 30 seconds, with two lifts. The first is 135 feet high with a 45-degree angle drop; the second is 141 feet high with a long steady drop of only 18 degrees that builds into a speed of 64.77 miles per hour before entering a 540-degree helix tunnel. The Beast has been the Guinness World Record holder for the world's longest wooden roller coaster since it opened.

VORTEX (1987)   Designed by Arrow Dynamics, this was the world's first coaster to have at least six inversions. It has two vertical loops, one double corkscrew, and one boomerang. Riding time is about 2½ minutes to cover the 3,200-foot-long track.

KING COBRA (1984)   This was America's first "stand-up" looping roller coaster. Designed by Togo, Inc., this steel coaster is 2,210 feet long and reaches a top speed of 50 miles per hour. It features a 360-degree vertical loop that is 66 feet high and a 540-degree horizontal loop that thrusts riders nearly parallel to the ground.

THE RACER (1972)   This coaster is generally acknowledged as having revived the interest in American wooden coasters. Designed by John Allen, this was originally a racing coaster with twin tracks straight out-and-back. In 1982 one of the trains was reversed so that it runs backward. The tracks are each 3,415 feet long and the ride takes approximately 2½ minutes, reaching a top speed of 61 miles per hour.

ADVENTURE EXPRESS (1991)   Arrow Dynamics designed this 2,963-foot-long mine train type coaster with two lifts, which are 63 feet and 42 feet high. During the 2½ minute ride, the train travels at 35 miles per hour through four themed tunnels.

TOP GUN (1993)   A 2,352-foot-long suspended coaster designed by Arrow Dynamics, this is a 1 minute, 30 second, 51 miles per hour ride that has a high point of 78 feet.

THE BEASTIE (1972)   This juvenile "Beast" is a 1,350-foot-long wooden coaster designed by the Philadelphia Toboggan Company. The ride time is one and a half minutes.

TOP CAT'S TAXI JAM (1992)   One of the Miler Coaster Company's junior steel rides. The 199 feet of track is covered in 55 seconds.

OUTER LIMITS: FLIGHT OF FEAR (1996)   The first coaster in the United

King Cobra (Paramount's Kings Island).

Top: The Racer. Bottom: Adventure Express (Paramount's Kings Island).

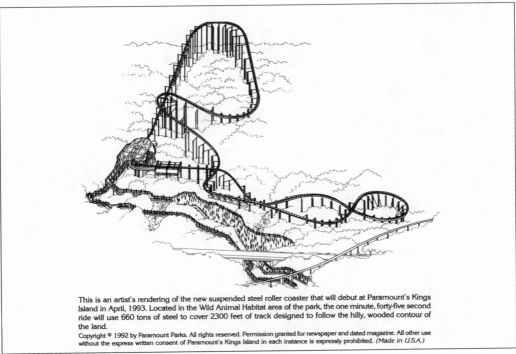

This is an artist's rendering of the new suspended steel roller coaster that will debut at Paramount's Kings Island in April, 1993. Located in the Wild Animal Habitat area of the park, the one minute, forty-five second ride will use 660 tons of steel to cover 2300 feet of track designed to follow the hilly, wooded contour of the land.

Top and Bottom: Top Gun (Paramount's Kings Island).

Face/Off (Paramount's Kings Island).

States to use linear induction motors, this Premier design launches riders from zero to 54 mph in less than four seconds. There are 2,705 feet of twisting, turning track with four inversions, all enclosed upon a one acre site. The ride time is just over one minute.

SCOOBY'S GHOSTER COASTER (1998)   Caripro Amusement Technology built this 450-foot-long suspended children's coaster. The first of its kind in North America, riders are taken up a vertical lift and then allowed to coast above Hanna-Barbera land for one minute.

FACE/OFF (1999)   Sitting face-to-face, with legs and feet dangling, this inverted Vekoma coaster follows 1,970 feet of track for one and a half minutes. Dropping 125 feet from the 138-foot-high lift at 55 mph through three inversions forward and backwards. Riders on this roller coaster will feel 5 G's.

SON OF BEAST (2000)   For the sequel to the Beast, Paramount's Kings Island just had two requirements: 1. The "Son" must be a "terrain coaster" that follows the hilly land contours. 2. This wooden coaster must have a single vertical loop. Absent for the better part of a century, the wooden coaster loop returns with the engineering and design efforts of the Roller Coaster Corporation of America and Werner Stengel.

This two year project began with 12 hilly acres and more than 312 miles

Space Rocket Train (Americana Amusement Park).

The Screechin' Eagle (Americana Amusement Park).

The Screechin' Eagle (Americana Amusement Park).

of Southern Yellow Pine lumber resulting in several world's records for a wooden coaster. The tallest structure ever built (218 feet), the longest drop (214 feet) and the world's fastest (78 mph). At 164 feet, the second drop is the second tallest drop in the world and there is yet another incredible drop of almost 150 feet on this 7,032-foot-long track (the second longest wooden coaster in the world). The interior height of the loop is 103 feet with a 118-foot-high steel superstructure supporting this portion of the wooden track. The three minute ride also includes two 540-degree helices, one curving left, the other curving right. The investment is more than it took to build the entire park.

Americana Amusement Park
5757 Middletown-Hamilton Road
Middletown, Ohio 45044

Opened in 1922, Americana was known as Lesordsville Lake Amusement Park until 1978. Today the 65-acre park is owned by the Coney Island Group Company of Cincinnati, Ohio.

THE SCREECHIN' EAGLE (1927)   Designed and built by John Miller in Zanesville, Ohio, this wooden out-and-back is known for "airtime." The first drop is 78 feet at 45 mph, beginning a 2,640-foot-long ride that lasts for 1 minute, 30 seconds. The coaster was brought to Lesordsville in 1938 and named the Comet, then in 1960 it was renamed the Space Rocket. Finally, in 1978 both the coaster and the park were given their current names.

THE SERPENT (1972)   Relocated here in 1988, this spiraling 1,640-foot-long steel figure-eight has a first drop of 62 feet and darts along at speeds up to 30 mph.

THE LITTLE DIPPER   This Allen Herschell kiddie coaster has an 18-foot lift and 100 feet of steel track.

Wyandot Lake
10101 Riverside Drive
Powell, Ohio 43065
www.wyandotlake.com

Cedar Point (Dan Feicht).

A combination of traditional amusement park and waterpark, this facility is now owned and operated by Premier Parks.

SEA DRAGON (1956)   Considered an ideal first roller coaster experience for children, this old woodie is 35 feet tall and 1,320 feet long. The first coaster ever designed by John Allen of the Philadelphia Toboggan Company, Sea Dragon runs one minute, thirty seconds.

Cedar Point
P.O. Box 5006
Sandusky, Ohio 44871-8006
www.cedarpoint.com

This park, on the banks of Lake Erie, first opened in 1870. It is particularly known for its roller coaster lineup with more coasters than any other park in North America. The first coaster to appear at the Point was the Switchback Railway in 1892. Since that time this park has contained almost every type of coaster. During the 1950s, the last of the old coasters were dismantled as part of a park revitalization program that essentially cleared the way for today's coasters.

The Blue Streak (Dan Feicht).

THE BLUE STREAK (1964)   Built by the Philadelphia Toboggan Company, this is the oldest coaster in the park. It is a fast and hilly, straight out-and-back. It takes only 1 minute, 45 seconds to cover the 2,558-foot-long track at a top speed of 40 miles per hour. The first drop is from 78 feet and at an angle of 45 degrees. The loading station is located on a curve, rather than a straight section like most.

CEDAR CREEK MINE RIDE (1969)   One of the first runaway mine train–type rides designed by Arrow Dynamics to go into operation, its steel track is 2,540 feet long with a lift height of 48 feet. This coaster is relatively tame during its 2 minute, 42 second run.

WILDCAT (1970)   The Wildcat has fast, sharp turns and brightly colored cars, which hold only four passengers each. This makes the rider feel a bit more independent, adding even more excitement to the experience. Tight curves, frequent dips, and the rumble of wheels and gusts of breeze created by other cars as they pass around you accent the feel of the ride. It has an overlapping and interlocking figure-eight metal track configuration by Anton Schwarzkopf. At a height of 50 feet and 1,837 feet in length, the ride lasts for 1 minute, 25 seconds.

CORKSCREW (1976)   The world's first triple-looping coaster (two helical curves and a 360-degree vertical loop) by Arrow Dynamics. At 2,050 feet in length with an 85-foot-high lift, the ride takes 2 minutes, 15 seconds. It gains a speed off the first hill of 48 miles per hour that slows to 38 miles per hour within the eye of the corkscrew. And for those who would rather observe, the corkscrew offers a great view as it rumbles over the main pathway.

GEMINI (1978)   A unique combination of wood and steel, this coaster was the world's tallest and fastest when it first opened. Designed by Arrow, this is a racing coaster with twin parallel tracks in a figure-eight configuration. It is 3,935 feet in length and speeds up to 60 miles per hour in its 2 minute, 20 second running time. A 125-foot lift hill with a 55-degree slope begins a quick, smooth ride, which remains the most popular at Cedar Point.

IRON DRAGON (1987)   Cars are suspended below the track as they soar through S-curves and spirals, swinging out between the trees due to the forces of gravity. Two chain lifts and several dips take passengers from treetop heights to skimming just above the surface of a lagoon. A final tangle of track pulls riders through a pretzel-knot loop shrouded by mist. This is an Arrow design with two lifts of 76 feet and 62 feet that enable the train to reach 35–40 miles per hour. It takes approximately 2 minutes to cover the 2,800-foot-long track.

Corkscrew (Dan Feicht).

Top: Gemini. Bottom: The Mean Streak (Dan Feicht).

Magnum XL-200 (Dan Feicht).

The Mean Streak (Dan Feicht).

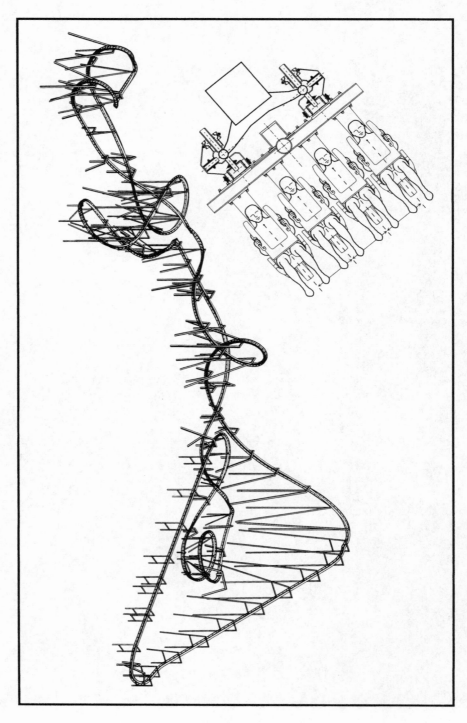

Raptor (Cedar Point).

MAGNUM **XL-200** (1989)   A traditional out-and-back but made entirely of steel, the XL-200 was designed by Arrow Dynamics with an $8 million price tag. It is listed in the 1990 *Guinness Book of World Records* as the fastest coaster with the longest drop. The first hill climbs 205 feet above the ground and plunges 194 feet, 8 inches, allowing the train to reach speeds of 72 miles per hour. The second hill drops riders from 157 feet and curves just in time to avoid Lake Erie. Along the way there are also three tunnels with special sound and lighting effects. The track is 5,105 feet long and the ride time is around 2½ minutes. Also worth noting is the first drop at 60 degrees, making it as steep as any in the world.

THE MEAN STREAK (1991)   One of the world's tallest wooden coasters at 160 feet features a 52-degree, 155-foot first drop. The second of twelve hills is taller than most at 124 feet. Designed by Curtis D. Summers and constructed by the Dinn Corporation, this 5,427-foot-long oblong-shaped course is traced three times in 2 minutes, 20 seconds. Weaving in and out of the structure, the train can reach a top speed of 65 miles per hour.

RAPTOR (1994)   This inverted steel coaster was designed by Bolliger & Mabillard as the world's tallest, longest and fastest of its kind. From a lift of 137 feet the train drops 119 feet at a speed of 57 mph. The 3,790-foot-long ride takes 2 minutes, 16 seconds.

Millennium Force (Cedar Point).

Cedar Creek Mine Ride (Dan Feicht).

Mantis (Dan Feicht).

MANTIS (1996)   One of the tallest, fastest and steepest stand-up roller coasters in the world. Bolliger & Mabillard designed this $12 million, two and a half minute ride. With 3,900 feet of track and a lift height of 145 feet, the "bystanders" travel 60 mph down the 137-foot first drop.

WOODSTOCK'S EXPRESS (1999)   Designed by Vekoma, this family steel roller coaster is 1,100 feet in length, 38 feet tall and reaches speeds of only 25 mph during the one minute and forty second run.

JR. GEMINI (1979)   A tubular steel figure-eight designed specifically for children by Intamin. This 50 second, 6 mph ride requires that adults be accompanied by a child!

MILLENNIUM FORCE (2000)   The first roller coaster in history to top 300 feet is designed by Intamin AG of Wollerau, Switzerland, and described as a "giga-coaster." This steel out-and-back set three world's records: the tallest at 310 feet, the fastest at 92 mph and the longest drop of a coaster at 300-feet. Using an elevator cable system, the train climbs a 45-degree lift hill and then has a swift descent at an 80-degree angle (only 10 degrees off of being straight down) beginning a two minute and forty-five second ride over 6,595 feet of brilliant blue track. The trains offer tiered seating for unobstructed views with the second row of seats in each car being slightly elevated. Additionally there are two long tunnels, a second hill of 169 feet and a third of 182 feet.

Frontier City
11501 Northeast Expressway
Oklahoma City, Oklahoma 73131
www.frontiercity.com

Extensively themed as an 1880s frontier town, this relatively small facility opened in 1958 and is the origin and corporate headquarters of Premier Parks amusement park empire.

SILVER BULLET (1979)   This 1,942-foot-long coaster found its home here in 1986 after appearances at the Texas State Fair and Jolly Roger Park. Designed by Anton Schwarzkopf, the lift is 83 feet high, which gives the train a 55 mile per hour speed into the single loop. Total ride time is 1 minute, 15 seconds.

WILDCAT (1968)   Moved here in 1991, this was the last coaster designed by

Wildcat (Frontier City).

Silver Bullet (Frontier City).

National Amusement Devices. Originally located in Kansas City, this woodie was reconfigured to include a splashdown finale similar to Disneyland's Matterhorn. Statistically, the 2,653-foot-long ride has a 75-foot-high lift, a 65-foot drop, and reaches speeds of 50 miles per hour during its 2 minute run.

NIGHTMARE (1977)   This S.D.C. windstorm was introduced here in 1989. Enclosed in complete darkness, the 20 mph ride seems much faster as it follows the twisting, turning roller coaster track.

DIAMOND BACK (1978)   One of the Arrow Dynamic shuttle loop coasters originally located at Six Flags Great Adventure. Introduced here in 1994, the highlight of this 45 mph ride is a vertical loop that the train is propelled into, both forward and backward.

WILD KITTY (1991)   This is an Allen Herschell junior steel coaster around 100 feet long.

Bell's Amusement Park
3901 E. 21st Street
Tulsa, Oklahoma 74114

Robert K. Bell, Sr., opened his park in 1951 on the corner of the Tulsa State Fairgrounds. During the fair's two week run, this 10 acre facility becomes a major part of the midway.

ZINGO (1968)   Reflecting on his childhood memories, Robert Bell, Sr., named this wooden coaster after the Zingo Cannon Ball from the defunct Crystal City Amusement Park. Clearing a couple of hurdles, but restricted on operating hours, the 2,560-foot-long out-and-back opened on July 10. John Allen designed this 90 second ride, highlighted with a lift of 72 feet and a third drop of 74 feet at 50 mph that bottoms out 22 feet underground.

Enchanted Forest
8462 Enchanted Way SE
Turner, Oregon 97392
www.enchantedforest.com

Ice Mountain Bobsled (Enchanted Forest).

After seven years of construction this fantasy park opened in August 1971.

ICE MOUNTAIN BOBSLED (1983)   Designed by Roger Tofte and Dave Windows, this 1,400-foot-long steel coaster is an original with an undulating, turning course down a mountainside. The 2½ minute ride includes two lifts and has a top speed of 27 mph.

Dorney Park
3830 Dorney Park Road
Allentown, Pennsylvania 18104
www.dorneypark.com

Solomon Dorney opened this park in 1884 as "Dorney's Trout Ponds and Summer Resort." In 1901, the Allentown-Kutztown Traction Company purchased the park as was common with many trolley companies during this period. Today Cedar Fair L.P. owns and operates this historical park, one of the few survivors from the turn of the "other" century.

Thunderhawk (Dorney Park).

THUNDERHAWK (1923)   Originally designed as an out-and-back by Herbert Schmeck of the Philadelphia Toboggan Company, this 2,767-foot-long wooden roller coaster was changed into a figure-eight layout in 1930. Known simply as "the coaster" until 1989, this 45 mph ride starts from an 80-foot-high lift and weaves its way through the trees of a picnic area during its 1 minute, 18 second run.

LAZER (1986)   This double-looping steel coaster was designed by Anton Schwarzkopf as a portable model. It has a 90-foot lift and a top speed of 50 miles per hour. The 2,200-foot-long track is covered in 1 minute, 30 seconds.

HERCULES (1989)   The train leaves the station and immediately drops 55 feet before climbing the 95-foot lift hill which leads to a surprising 157-foot drop. Following the natural contours, Curtis Summers designed this 4,000-foot-long terrain coaster with the world's longest wooden drop at the time. The two minute ride reaches speeds of 60 mph.

STEEL FORCE (1997)   Designed by D.H. Morgan Manufacturing, this "hyper-coaster" is a steel out-and-back with a first drop of 205 feet and a top speed of 75 mph. During the three minute ride over 5,600-feet of track, you will encounter two tunnels, a 510-degree helix and four "camelbacks" for that special airtime.

THE LITTLE LAZER (1991)   A children's steel coaster great for beginners.

WILD MOUSE (2000)   Designed by Maurer-Sohne, this steel coaster is a zig-zagging thriller that teases you at every hairpin turn.

Lakemont Park
700 Park Avenue
Altoona, Pennsylvania 16602

Opening in 1894, Lakemont Park is the only place you can take a ride back in time — on the oldest standing roller coaster in the world.

LEAP-THE-DIPS (1902)   On May 31, 1999, this historical roller coaster became operational once again. Since 1985, the ride had sat dormant, slowly deteriorating until a determined effort led by the American Coaster Enthusiasts (ACE) took on the task of raising the funds necessary to begin

Lazer (Dorney Park).

Hercules (Dorney Park).

Steel Force (Dorney Park).

The Little Lazer (Dorney Park).

Top: Leap-the-Dips. Bottom: Skyliner (Lakemont Park).

restoration. Designed by E. Joy Morris, it is the only remaining "side friction figure-eight," which was very popular from about 1900 until 1920. It is believed to be the world's oldest standing coaster. It stands 48 feet tall at its highest point and has a series of gentle slopes along its 1,980 feet of track. Considering that this type of ride had essentially become obsolete by the beginning of the 1920s, it is truly remarkable that one has survived.

SKYLINER (1965)   Originally built by John Allen and the Philadelphia Toboggan Company, this 3,500-foot-long L-shaped wooden coaster was relocated in 1985 from Roseland Park in Canandaigua, New York. Completely refurbished by Charles Dinn, the Skyliner begins the one minute and twenty-five second ride from a 110-foot lift at 60 mph down a 96-foot drop.

Conneaut Lake Park
12382 Center Street
Conneaut Lake, Pennsylvania 16316
www.visitcrawford.org/clp1.html

This is an old traditional lakeside amusement park that opened in 1892.

BLUE STREAK (1937)   This famous coaster was designed by Ed Vettel and is especially noted for its unique "camel humps"— a series of three dramatic hills that occur in breathtakingly quick succession on the "out" side of the ride's 2,900-foot-long circuit. The wooden structure has a lift hill 78 feet tall and takes 2 minutes, 5 seconds to ride. It is also well known for its "Skunk Tunnel" named in recognition of the numerous times that a coaster train has met a skunk or two in the tunnel that begins the ride, to the mutual dismay and lasting impression of all parties involved.

Knoebels Amusement Resort
P.O. Box 317
Elysburg, Pennsylvania 17824
www.knoebels.com

"Knoebels Grove" was attracting visitors to the swimming hole long before the amusement park was established in 1926.

PHOENIX (1947)   Originally designed by Herbert Schmeck, this wooden out-and-back was moved here in 1985 from San Antonio Playland ("Rocket") by Charles Dinn. The 2 minute, 10 second ride has a 2,300-foot-long track, a 78-foot-high lift, and a top speed of 45 miles per hour.

Top: Phoenix (Terry Wild Studio). Bottom: Twister (Knoebels Amusement Resort).

Twister (Knoebels Amusement Resort).

WHIRLWIND (1984)   This is a steel corkscrew designed by Vekoma that was moved here from Playland Park, Rye, New York, in 1993. To make room, the Jet Star was sold to Morey's Pier in Wildwood, New Jersey.

HIGH SPEED THRILL COASTER (1955)   This 18-foot-tall, 200-foot-long junior steel coaster is believed to be the only one built by the Overland Amusement Company still in operation.

TWISTER (1999)   When Elitch Gardens relocated in 1995, they left behind a classic coaster in "Mr. Twister." Using the original plans by John Allen and the Philadelphia Toboggan Company, John Fetterman adapted a new twister to Knoebels' site with a few modifications. This new woodie is 3,900 feet long with a 101-foot lift and an 89-foot first drop. The two minute and ten second ride will remind you of Colorado.

Waldameer Park
P.O. Box 8308
Erie, Pennsylvania 16505
www.waldameer.com

Located on the shores of Lake Erie, this site was originally known as Hoffman's Grove until the Lake Erie Traction Company leased it in 1896. Renamed Waldameer, which in German means "woods by the sea," the trolley park began a series of expansions including the 1920s Ravine Flyer which was demolished in 1938.

COMET (1951)   Designed by Herbert Schmeck of the Philadelphia Toboggan Company, this wooden coaster begins with a 45-foot lift and runs along 1,400 feet of track before returning to the rare curved loading station.

Hersheypark
100 West Hersheypark Drive
Hershey, Pennsylvania 17033-0866
www.hersheypark.com

Comet (Hersheypark).

Hersheypark opened in 1907 and personifies the clean, green playground escape that Milton Hershey designed for his hard-working chocolate factory employees. The park is located in a town with history as rich as its chocolate. Tree-lined streets, wide open spaces, and services were created to meet the resident's every need. Today, the town's quaint country atmosphere, inspiring beauty, and many attractions make Hershey a treasured vacation spot.

COMET (1946)   This wooden coaster was designed by Herb Schmeck, built by the Philadelphia Toboggan Company, and replaced the Wildcat coaster. Although still a wood structure, the 3,360-foot-long track was replaced with a steel track in 1978. The riding time is 1 minute, 45 seconds, and the train can reach a top speed of 50 miles per hour from a first lift of 78 feet.

SOOPERDOOPERLOOPER (1977)   Designed by Anton Schwarzkopf, this was the first steel loop coaster to be located on the East Coast. The 2,614-foot-long track has a lift hill of 70 feet and one vertical loop 57 feet in height. Riding time is 1 minute, 30 seconds.

TRAIL BLAZER COASTER (1974)   A runaway mine train type with steel track, 1,874 feet long, designed by Arrow Dynamics.

SIDEWINDER (1992)   Designed by Vekoma, this is a steel boomerang type. The train is pulled backward to the top of a nearly vertical eleven-story tower, then released going 55 miles per hour into a butterfly section and one vertical loop. The train comes to a rest momentarily at the top of another tower before making the same trip again — only backward!

GREAT BEAR (1998)   An inverted looping coaster designed by Bolliger & Mabillard that takes passengers along 2,800 feet of track for 2 minutes and 55 seconds. The experience has been compared to riding an out of control ski lift at 60 mph.

THE WILDCAT (1996)   Designed by Great Coasters International, this wooden cyclone coaster is 3,100 feet long and has a lift hill of 85-feet. With a maximum speed of 49 mph, the ride is 1 minute and 15 seconds.

THE WILD MOUSE (1999)   This "Mad Mouse" type of coaster is appropriately located in the fair section. You will serpentine through the 1,214-foot-long Mack designed course teetering on the edge of every corner during this two minute ride.

LIGHTNING RACER (2000)   A racing, "dueling" wooden coaster described as a hybrid (blend of cyclone and out-and-back) designed by Great Coasters International. From 100 feet high, the two tracks race side by side before splitting off to begin the face-to-face duel. With 15 drops and 3400 feet of intertwining track each, the two trains fly by each other often within six feet. This $12.5 million coaster concludes the two minute and twenty second race with a close encounter of a rushing waterfall.

Comet (Hersheypark).

SooperDooperLooper (Hershey Park).

Top: Trail Blazer Coaster. Bottom: Sidewinder (Hershey Park).

Top: Great Bear (Hersheypark). Bottom: The Wildcat (Great Coasters International).

Lightning Racer (Hersheypark).

Dutch Wonderland

2249 Route 30 East
Lancaster, Pennsylvania 17602-1188
www.dutchwonderland.com

Located in the heart of Pennsylvania Dutch Amish country, this amusement park opened in 1963.

THE SKY PRINCESS (1992)   This 2,000-foot-long wooden out-and-back was designed by Custom Coaster, Inc., and installed in just four months. It has a lift of 55 feet, speeds of 40 miles per hour, and lasts for 90 seconds.

THE JOUST (1998)   This small steel coaster was designed for the entire family.

Idlewild Park

P.O. Box C
Ligonier, Pennsylvania 15658
www.idlewild.com

Referred to as America's most beautiful park, Idlewild opened in 1878 as a stop on the Ligonier Valley Railroad's narrow gauge line. Acquired by the Kennywood Park

The Sky Princess (Mike Rieker).

Corporation in 1983, this place is also the home of Mister Rogers' Neighborhood of Make-Believe.

ROLLO COASTER (1938)   The Philadelphia Toboggan Company designed and built this 1,400-foot-long wooden out-and-back. From a lift of 40 feet this classic runs over rolling hills and little dips for 1 minute, 10 seconds. Legend has it that the wood for the structure was cut from trees on site.

WILD MOUSE (1988)   Relocated here in 1993 from Alton Towers in England, the steel wild mouse is 1,640 feet long and 56 feet high. This Vekoma design has sudden hairpin turns which give individual four seat cars the illusion of flying over the edge.

Williams Grove Amusement Park

One Park Avenue
Mechanicsburg, Pennsylvania 17055
www.williamsgrove.com

The Sky Princess (Dutch Wonderland).

A 350-acre traditional amusement park that opened in 1850 and located in a rural area of Pennsylvania, this place takes advantage of its natural setting.

CYCLONE (1933)   Originally called the Zipper, this is a classic double-decker wooden out-and-back with 2,300 feet of track designed by the Philadelphia Toboggan Company.

Kennywood
4800 Kennywood Boulevard
West Mifflin, Pennsylvania 15122
www.kennywood.com

The park opened in 1898 and was designated a National Historic Landmark in 1987, with beautiful gardens, fountains, and shade trees. Kennywood is rich in roller coaster history. Today there are five major coasters: three wooden and two steel.

JACK RABBIT (1922)   In 1921, one of America's top coaster firms, Miller and Baker, was hired to design a new high speed coaster. John A. Miller designed the $50,000 coaster by taking advantage of a ravine on the edge of the park and thereby using less lumber. A new system of wheels under the track was implemented to allow for the creation of a 70-foot-high double dip. In 1947, a tunnel after the first drop was removed and the original trains were replaced with ones built by Andy Vettel's uncle, Ed Vettel of West View Park. The entire wooden coaster is 2,132 feet long with a 70-foot-high lift.

THE RACER (1927)   The park's original was built in 1910 as a wooden twin-track racing coaster, which was the world's largest at the time. It did not have wheels under the track, so dips and curves had to be gentle. The new Racer had wheels under the tracks, which permitted banked curves as well as curves on the dips. In his design, John A. Miller, of Miller and Baker, included a reverse curve so the train that started on the right side of the loading platform would finish on the left side. The length of the track is 2,250 feet and it has a lift of 72 feet.

THUNDERBOLT (1968)   Designed by Andy Vettel, this ride has a 95-foot-high lift and is 2,887 feet long. It was built around and incorporated the first and last drops and a tunnel of the old Pippin (1924–1967), which was designed by John A. Miller. The Thunderbolt is unusual in that it starts with a drop into a ravine and does not reach the first lift until the ride is half over. This coaster is also well known for its 90-foot final drop.

STEEL PHANTOM (1991)   Using the existing terrain, Arrow Dynamics designed a coaster for Kennywood with several elements that have become

Jack Rabbit (Kennywood).

The Racer (Kennywood).

synonymous with the steel coaster. The 3,000-foot-long track includes a twisting first drop from a 160-foot lift that leads to the second hill's drop, which has been described as "the thrill of a lifetime." Taking advantage of the natural topography, this drop is one of the world's longest at 225 feet, bringing the train to a speed of 80 miles per hour. This is followed by four inversions, a vertical loop, boomerang, and corkscrew. All of this action occurs within 1 minute, 45 seconds.

LIL' PHANTOM (1996)   Only 154 feet long, this small steel junior roller coaster is designed specifically for the kids.

THE EXTERMINATOR (1999)   This is a 1,400-foot-long wild mouse–like track layout extensively themed within an enclosed environment. Designed by Reverchon Industries of Paris, France, this ride has a lift of 50 feet and navigates hairpin turns at 20 mph during its three minute run.

Thunderbolt (Kennywood).

Steel Phantom (Kennywood).

Top: Steel Phantom/Thunderbolt. Bottom: The Exterminator (Kennywood).

Family Kingdom Amusement Park

300 4th Avenue South
Myrtle Beach, South Carolina 29577
www.familykingdom.com

Located along the famous Grand Strand, this park offers a variety of amusements including the largest wooden roller coaster in South Carolina.

SWAMP FOX (1966)   Dropping from 75 feet, passengers coast along at up to 50 mph on this beautiful white undulating structure that doubles out-and-back with 2,600 feet of track. Designed by John Allen of the Philadelphia Toboggan Company, this wooden coaster was given new life in 1992 with the opening of Family Kingdom.

Myrtle Beach Pavilion Amusement Park

812 N. Ocean Blvd.
Myrtle Beach, South Carolina 29577
www.mbpavilion.com

Located in the heart of downtown Myrtle Beach, this 11-acre amusement park first opened in 1949.

THE CORKSCREW (1975)   Designed by Arrow Dynamics and relocated here in 1978, this 1,250-foot-long steel corkscrew is one of the first to turn riders upside down in the modern era.

MAD MOUSE (1998)   The innocent ascent to the top of this zig-zagging steel track might lull you into false complacency, but once at the top each threatening hairpin turn will leave you gasping.

LITTLE EAGLE (1985)   This is a small steel roller coaster designed by Mack for the beginners.

HURRICANE CATEGORY 5 (2000)   The first wooden roller coaster to be built at the pavilion is a 110-foot-tall combination out-and-back /twister designed by Custom Coasters International. A 3,800-foot-long track with a galvanized steel support structure, you can whiteknuckle this one all you want — there will be no evacuation!

Libertyland

940 Early Maxwell Boulevard
Memphis, Tennessee 38104
www.libertyland.com

Located in the center of Memphis at the mid-south fairgrounds, this park opened on the fourth of July in 1976 in honor of the nation's bicentennial.

REVOLUTION (1979)   This is one of the steel double corkscrew coasters designed by Arrow Dynamics with an additional vertical loop that is 75 feet high. It takes 1 minute, 20 seconds to ride the 1,565-foot-long coaster.

ZIPPIN PIPPIN (1915)   Re-built by the National Amusement Device Company of Dayton, Ohio, this is one of the oldest operating wooden roller coasters in North America and is said to have been a favorite of Elvis Presley. The ride first opened in 1915 in the old East End in the Overton Square section of Memphis, but was brought to the old fairgrounds park in 1923 and rebuilt at a cost of $45,000. At this time its travel flow was changed to a figure-eight. It has a maximum drop of 70 feet and a length of 2,865 feet, and great care is taken to replace its wood every seven years to help preserve the structure.

Revolution (Libertyland).

Zippin Pippin (Libertyland).

Dollywood
1020 Dollywood Lane
Pigeon Forge, Tennessee 37863-4101
www.dollywood.com

Originally developed by Silver Dollar City, Inc., this park adopted a new image in 1986 with the partnership of Dolly Parton. Her Smoky Mountain heritage provided for the "homespun fun" environment.

BLAZING FURY (1977)   Designed in-house, this indoor coaster is comparable to a modern scenic railway. With a top speed of 35 mph, these steel tracks take you through a burning town with sudden drops up to 25 feet, including one with a splash.

TENNESSEE TORNADO (1999)   An $8 million Arrow Dynamics creation amidst the splendor of the Smoky Mountains. Climbing 137 feet, this adventure begins by dropping 128 feet straight through the mountain at 63 mph, then emerging into the first of four inversions. It takes 1 minute, 48 seconds to complete this 2,682-foot-long track which includes a signature "butterfly" section in honor of Dolly.

Tennessee Tornado (Dollywood).

Winston Cup Race World
250 Island Drive
Pigeon Forge, Tennessee 37863

A 20-acre family entertainment center located in the heart of this Smoky Mountain seasonal tourist mecca known as Pigeon Forge.

THE INTIMIDATOR (2000)   Designed by Coaster Works and named in honor of NASCAR's Dale Earnhardt, this 70-foot-tall out-and-back is the first wooden roller coaster to be built in the Pigeon Forge area.

Wonderland Park
2601 Dumas Dr. @ Thompson Park
Amarillo, Texas 79107
www.wonderlandpark.com

This park was first opened in 1951 in the city park on land leased from the city under the name of Kiddyland. Business grew fast and in 1967, the amusement park was incorporated under the name Wonderland.

TEXAS TORNADO (1985)   This coaster is a double-loop steel structure 80 feet tall and 2,050 feet long. An unusual-looking coaster, this was the first designed by O.D. Hopkins Associates, Inc. It has been referred to as a "Traver" experience due to its fast-paced course, which includes a 200-foot-long tunnel 13 feet under the ground.

Six Flags Over Texas
P.O. Box 90191
Arlington, Texas 76004-0191
www.sixflags.com

Located midway between Dallas and Fort Worth, the original Six Flags park opened in 1961. Its name was chosen for the six flags that have flown over Texas during the past. Originally, it was to be named "Texas Under Six Flags," but as the parks planners put it, "You know how we all feel about Texas, and Texas ain't never been under nothing." Thus it became Six Flags Over Texas.

TEXAS GIANT (1990)   This is one of the world's tallest wooden coasters at 143 feet. The 4,290-foot-long track begins with a 137-foot first drop at

Texas Tornado (Wonderland Park).

a 53-degree angle giving it a top speed of 62 miles per hour. This 2 minute ride was designed by Curtis D. Summers of Cincinnati and contains twenty-one drops, probably because this was his twenty-first coaster design.

JUDGE ROY SCREAM (1980) This is a classic wooden out-and-back designed as a family-oriented ride — in other words, exciting but not terrifying. It is 2,500 feet long with a 65-foot-high lift and can attain 53 miles per hour during its 2 minute run.

SHOCK WAVE (1978) This steel coaster by Intamin and Anton Schwarzkopf was the first to feature back-to-back loops. At the top of the 116-foot-high lift, the track curves gently before plunging toward the base of the first loop, which it enters into with a force of 5.9 G's at 60 miles per hour. It only takes about 2 minutes to cover the 3,500-foot-long track.

FLASHBACK (1989) On this steel boomerang with a vertical loop designed by Vekoma, the train is pulled up a 125-foot tall tower and then released to follow the track before stopping at the top of a second tower and then returning backwards.

RUNAWAY TRAIN (1966) This 2,400-foot-long coaster was the first of its kind. It was designed by Arrow Dynamics to give passengers the sensation of being aboard a mining ore train that had gone out of control.

Texas Giant (Six Flags Over Texas).

There are three lifts, the tallest of which is 35 feet high, and at one point the train travels through a tunnel under a lake.

RUNAWAY MOUNTAIN (1996)   Referred to as the coaster that dares the darkness, this one is housed within a 14,000-square-foot enclosure. Designed by Premier Rides the track is 1,378 feet long with no inversions and the maximum speed is 40 mph.

MR. FREEZE (1998)   Powered by 224 linear induction motors, Premier Rides designed this 1,480-foot-long steel coaster to reach 70 mph within 4 seconds. On opening day, Mr. Freeze was the tallest (236 feet) and fastest in Texas.

BATMAN: THE RIDE (1999)   The ski lift–style chairs suspended from the 2,700-foot-long track take riders through five inversions. Designed by Bolliger & Mabillard, this roller coaster has a 109-foot-high lift, a top speed of 50 mph and encounters up to 4 G's.

Texas Giant (Six Flags Over Texas).

Judge Roy Scream (Six Flags Over Texas).

Shock Wave (Six Flags Over Texas).

Flashback (Six Flags Over Texas).

Runaway Mountain (Premiere Rides, Inc.).

Mr. Freeze (Six Flags Over Texas).

Top: Mr. Freeze. Bottom: Batman: The Ride (Six Flags Over Texas).

Batman: The Ride (Six Flags Over Texas).

Six Flags Astroworld
9001 Kirby Drive
Houston, Texas 77054
www.sixflags.com

The park opened in 1968 under the ownership of Judge Roy Hofheinz and de-
rived its name from the inspiration of the nation's space program. In early 1975, the
park was sold to the Six Flags Corporation.

TEXAS CYCLONE (1976)   Designed by William Cobb, this coaster is mod-
eled after the famous Cyclone in Coney Island. It has a 93-foot-high lift
and can reach a top speed of 65 miles per hour while coasting over the
3,180-foot-long track. The first drop at a 53-degree angle is one of the
steepest on any coaster.

EXCALIBUR (1972)   This original roller coaster of the park is a tubular
steel track type designed by Arrow Dynamics. It has an 80-foot-high lift
with a 60-foot drop reaching a top speed of between 35–40 miles per
hour. Originally called the Dexter Frebish Roller Coaster, the name was
changed in 1981.

GREEZED LIGHTNIN' (1978)   A shuttleloop coaster by Anton Schwarzkopf
featuring an elliptical 360-degree loop. Riders are propelled from 0 to 60
miles per hour in 4 seconds, circle the 80-foot-high loop, then surge up
a near vertical 70-foot-tall incline before repeating the same ride backward.

XLR-8 (1984)   A hanging steel coaster designed by Arrow Dynamics. It
takes 3 minutes to cover the 3,000-foot-long track, which has a first lift
of 81 feet. This is one of the first successful suspended coasters following
"The Bat" (1981), which was the prototype in Cincinnati.

ULTRA TWISTER (1986)   This ride was moved from Six Flags Great Adventure and opened at Astroworld in 1990. Designed by Togo, Inc., this
unusual steel coaster is 1,181 feet long and has a lift of 96 feet. It can reach
43.5 miles per hour during its 1 minute, 40 second ride, through a forward run with one spin rotation and a backward run with a two spin rotation.

VIPER (1981)   This single-looping steel coaster created by Anton
Schwarzkopf was moved to the park in 1989 from Six Flags Over Mid-
America. The 1,968 feet of track has a high point of 80 feet, a top speed
of 50 mph and runs for one minute, thirty seconds.

BATMAN: THE ESCAPE (1987)   Originally located at Six Flags Magic
Mountain, then at Six Flags Great Adventure (1990–1992), the Shockwave
has relocated with a new name. This is the only stand-up looping coaster
designed by Intamin in North America. It is 2,300 feet long, 90 feet high,

Texas Cyclone (Six Flags Astroworld).

Ultra Twister (Six Flags Astroworld).

and achieves a top speed of 55 miles per hour while entering the 66-foot-high vertical loop.

THE SERPENT (1969)   One of the park's original coasters, this mini mine train is 770 feet long and was designed by Arrow Dynamics.

TEXAS TORNADO (1998)   From 112 feet, this Schwarzkopf coaster drops at 62 mph into a 3,280-foot-long track that twists, turns and loops for 2 minutes, 30 seconds. Formerly known as Taz's Texas Tornado.

SERIAL THRILLER (1999)   A suspended looping roller coaster by Vekoma with a total of five inversions. Feet dangling below from a 102-foot height, you plunge into the 2,172-foot-long course at 55 mph. The entire ride takes 1 minute, 35 seconds.

The Kiddie Park
3015 Broadway
San Antonio, Texas 78209

Viper (Six Flags Astroworld).

Established in 1925, this one acre amusement park is located in Brackenridge City Park and is the oldest children's facility of its kind in America.

LITTLE DIPPER (1950)   One of Allen Herschell's original kiddie coasters, this steel track layout is 12 feet tall, has a top speed of 18 mph and fits within a 40-foot by 100-foot space.

SeaWorld Adventure Park

10500 Sea World Drive
San Antonio, Texas 78251-3002
www.seaworld.com

Owned by Busch Entertainment Corporation, this is the largest marine life adventure park in the world. Since opening in 1988, several attractions have been added to the 250-acre facility, including the first roller coaster of any SeaWorld parks.

GREAT WHITE (1997)   Designed by Bolliger & Mabillard, this inverted steel coaster was the first of its kind in the state of Texas. With legs dangling from ski lift–style seats, riders encounter various inversions during

Great White (SeaWorld).

the 50 mph, two minute run. The overall length of the track is 2,562 feet, which includes a 108-foot-tall lift followed by an 81-foot drop.

THE STEEL EEL (1999)   This 3,700-foot-long steel hypercoaster gives plenty of "airtime" during its three minute journey. From a 150-foot first drop, the train hits 65 mph and undulates along an attractive out-and-back course designed by D.H. Morgan Manufacturing.

The Steel Eel (SeaWorld).

Six Flags Fiesta Texas
17000 I-10 West
San Antonio, Texas 78257
www.sixflags.com

Located in an old stone quarry, this park opened in March 1992 and was a partnership between subsidiaries of the USAA Insurance Company and Opryland USA, Inc. Sold to Six Flags, Fiesta Texas continues to expand.

RATTLER (1992)   Designed by John Pierce & Associates and built by the Roller Coaster Corporation of Texas, this mammoth coaster is built around a limestone quarry and includes tunnels within the quarry walls. It opened with four world records: the tallest wooden coaster structure at 180-feet, 6 inches; the longest first drop of any woodie at 166 feet, 4.5 inches (resulting in a gravitational pull of 3.5); fastest woodie, reaching a top speed of 73 miles per hour; and the steepest first drop of a wooden coaster at 61.4 degrees. The entire ride takes 2 minutes, 15 seconds, covering 5,080-feet of track.

DER ROLLERSCHUHCOASTER (1992)   A Vekoma "roller skater" that is a 679-foot-long smooth family coaster.

Rattler (Michael Murphy).

Boomerang (Six Flags Fiesta Texas).

Poltergeist (Six Flags Fiesta Texas).

JOKER'S REVENGE (1996)   This is a 1,936-foot-long, triple inversion steel design by Vekoma with a lift of 79 feet and a top speed of 40 mph.

ROADRUNNER EXPRESS (1997)   On steel track 2,400 feet long with a 73-foot lift, this is one of Arrow Dynamics' mine train–type roller coasters.

BOOMERANG (1999)   The classic Vekoma Coaster that begins from a 125-foot tower into a corkscrew/boomerang element followed by a vertical loop and then hesitates at the top of a second tower. Then it repeats backwards over 875 feet of track. The entire experience lasts 1 minute, 44 seconds.

POLTERGEIST (1999)   The linear induction motors launch the train from 0 to 60 mph in just 3.4 seconds into a "spaghetti" maze of track 2,705 feet long. Including four inversions, 30 vertical curves, this Premier Rides coaster reaches a height of 78 feet and runs for one minute, fifteen seconds.

Lagoon Park

375 N. Lagoon Drive
P.O. Box 696
Farmington, Utah 84025-0696
www.lagoonpark.com

This park opened on July 15, 1886, under the name Lake Park. In 1896, the resort was moved 2½ miles inland to its present location and the name was changed to suit its new location on the banks of a 9-acre lagoon.

THE ROLLER COASTER (1921)   Designed by John Miller, this is a traditional wooden coaster that is 2,500 feet long with a high point of 70 feet. It can reach a top speed of 45 miles per hour. In 1953, a fire at the park destroyed the front of the coaster, but it was soon rebuilt.

THE COLOSSAL FIRE DRAGON (1981)   A steel double loop designed by Anton Schwarzkopf, this ride is 85 feet high, 2,850 feet long, and can achieve 55 miles per hour during its 1 minute, 45 second run.

JET STAR (1974)   Approximately 2,000 feet long, this is another of Anton Schwarzkopf's designs — a smooth spiraling roller coaster.

PUFF THE ROLLER COASTER (1985)   A junior steel coaster created by Zierer, only 900 feet long with gentle speeds of 15 mph.

WILD MOUSE (1998)   Manufactured by Maurer-Sohne, this 1,200-foot-long coaster lifts 50 feet and then serpentines seven hairpin turns before dropping at 28 mph.

Top: The Roller Coaster. Bottom: The Colossal Fire Dragon (Lagoon Park).

Paramount's Kings Dominion
16000 Theme Park Way
Doswell, Virginia 23047-2000
www.pkdthrills.com

In 1975, the people of Kings Island opened this park and in 1983, Kings Entertainment Company (KECO) was formed, consisting of Kings Dominion, Carowinds, Kings Island, and Canada's Wonderland in Toronto. Currently, KECO owns Kings Dominion, Carowinds, Great America in Santa Clara, and 20 percent of Canada's Wonderland. In 1992, KECO was sold to Paramount Studios.

SHOCKWAVE (1986)   This is a tubular steel coaster in which riders are secured in a standing position. It is 2,210 feet long and reaches a top speed of 50 miles per hour, featuring a 360-degree vertical loop that is 66 feet high and a 540-degree horizontal loop that thrusts riders nearly parallel to the ground. Shockwave was designed by Togo, Inc., of Japan.

REBEL YELL (1975)   A wooden twin racing coaster, each track is 3,368 feet in length. The first of twelve hills is 87 feet high and the top speed is 65 miles per hour during its 2 minute, 15 second run.

THE GRIZZLY (1982)   This is an old-fashioned classic wooden coaster with a lift hill of 87 feet. The 3,150-foot-long track was patterned after Coney Island's Wildcat with a double figure-eight configuration. The entire ride is 2 minutes, 20 seconds.

ANACONDA (1991)   Designed by Arrow Dynamics, this steel coaster takes riders for a loop six times. From a 130-foot-high lift over a lake, the train plunges 144 feet into a tight underwater tunnel, pops back out and into the first of several loops. The length of this coaster is 2,700 feet, featuring the first butterfly configuration in the United States. It has a top speed of 50 miles per hour.

THE HURLER (1994)   Designed by International Coaster, Inc., this 3,157-foot-long woodie is themed for the "Wayne's World" section and is identical to the one at Paramount's Carowinds.

SCOOBY DOO (1974)   A John Allen (PTC) wooden junior coaster with a 1,385-foot-long track that doubles back on itself.

THE OUTER LIMITS: FLIGHT OF FEAR (1996)   Premier Rides' first linear induction suspended coaster propels riders from 0 to 54 mph within four seconds. Through 2,600 feet of enclosed track including four inversions, this ride operates completely in the dark.

TAXI JAM COASTER (1997)   A 200-foot-long junior steel coaster by the Miler Company. This is the perfect ride for young beginners.

VOLCANO, THE BLAST COASTER (1998)   Designed in-house and manufactured by Intamin AG, this 2,757-foot-long creation is the world's fastest

Shockwave (Paramount's Kings Dominion).

suspended roller coaster at 70 mph. With the use of electro-magnetic energy, riders will pass through four inversions while at times feeling the effect of 5 G's.

Rebel Yell (Paramount's Kings Dominion).

The Grizzly (Paramount's Kings Dominion).

Top: Anaconda. Bottom: Volcano, The Blast Coaster (Paramount's Kings Dominion).

Busch Gardens Williamsburg

One Busch Gardens Boulevard
Williamsburg, Virginia 23187-8785
www.buschgardens.com

Opening in 1975, this park is owned and operated by Busch Entertainment Corporation, one of the Anheuser-Busch companies. Its theme links the early American heritage of nearby Colonial Williamsburg with its European roots, featuring eight authentically detailed hamlets.

THE BIG BAD WOLF (1984)   A 2,800-foot-long hanging coaster designed by Arrow Dynamics, the 3 minute ride includes two lifts of 50 feet and 100 feet, the second of which brings the suspended trains to the top of a cliff before they dive 80 feet toward a lake. At this point the train reaches a top speed of 48 miles per hour just before being whipped to the left to avoid slapping the water.

THE LOCHNESS MONSTER (1978)   The first tubular steel coaster with interlocking loops, designed by Arrow Dynamics, its first drop is 114.2 feet

The Big Bad Wolf (Copyright © 1999 Busch Entertainment Corporation. Reproduced by permission of Busch Gardens Williamsburg. All rights reserved).

The Lochness Monster (Copyright © 1999 Busch Entertainment Corporation. Reproduced by permission of Busch Gardens Williamsburg. All rights reserved).

at 55 degrees. The speed during this drop accelerates from 12 to more than 60 miles per hour in just 2½ seconds, resulting in a G-force of 3.5. Between the two loops there is a tunnel containing a spiraling track 40 feet in diameter. The entire track is 3,240 feet long, and the ride lasts 2 minutes, 10 seconds.

APOLLO'S CHARIOT (1999)   Bolliger & Mabillard designed this 4,882-foot-long hypercoaster with nine "camel backs." These drops measured in feet are 210/131/144/102/48/87/38/16/49, the first of which leads to 73 mph and a 4.1 G-force. Sitting four across on elevated seats, passengers feel a "free-flight" sensation for the two minute duration of this ride.

ALPENGEIST (1997)   Named after a mountain ghost that stalks the German and French Alps, this inverted steel roller coaster is 3,828-feet-long and has a "ski" lift of 195 feet with a drop of 170 feet. Through six inversions at speeds up to 67 mph, this Bolliger & Mabillard design opened as the world's tallest of this type.

THE WILDE MAUS (1996)   Originally called "Wild Izzy" in honor of the Centennial Olympic Games, this mouse covers 1,217 feet of track. For 1 minute, 30 seconds, this Mack designed steel coaster navigates hairpin turns, 46 feet above the ground, at 22 miles per hour.

Top and Bottom: Alpengeist (Copyright © 1999 Busch Entertainment Corporation. Reproduced by permission of Busch Gardens Williamsburg. All rights reserved).

The Wilde Maus (Copyright © 1999 Busch Entertainment Corporation. Reproduced by permission of Busch Gardens Williamsburg. All rights reserved).

Puyallup Fair

P.O. Box 430
Puyallup, Washington 98371

In addition to the Roller Coaster, there is a 500-foot-long Miller Wild Mouse and the 1,837-foot-long steel Wildcat by Schwarzkopf. Because these coasters are part of the Puyallup Fair, they only operate two weeks a year.

ROLLER COASTER (1935)   The original layout by John Miller was destroyed by fire in the 1940s. Walter Leroy then redesigned the coaster in 1950 with a 55-foot-high lift and a double-out-and-back course, 2,650 feet in length. The 2 minute ride was also reconfigured to accommodate original Prior and Church Trains, the only ones of their kind still in operation.

Camden Park

P.O. Box 1778
500 Waverly Road
Huntington, West Virginia 25718
www.camdenpark.com

Roller Coaster (Puyallup Fair).

Named for Senator Johnson Newlon Camden, this traditional park has been enjoyed since 1903. Although it has evolved over the years, the feeling evoked is that of stepping back in time.

BIG DIPPER (1958)   This wooden coaster is an expanded figure-eight, 1,800 feet long with a 50-foot lift. National Amusement Devices is the designer of this classic ride.

LITTLE DIPPER (1961)   The much smaller version by National Amusement Devices has a 17-foot lift and 450 feet of wooden track supported by a steel structure.

Little A-Merrick-A
700 E. Main Street
Marshall, Wisconsin 53559

Owned by Lee Merrick, this park opened in 1990. Along with the miniature golf, go karts and roller coasters they feature a 16" gauge light railroad.

LITTLE DIPPER (1950)   This small Allen Herschell steel coaster was relocated and restored here in 1993.

MAD MOUSE (1960)   Bought from Enchanted Forest (Chesterton, Indiana) in 1992, this Herschell classic is enjoying a resurgence in popularity.

TOBOGGAN (1969)   The original! Chance built this 450-foot-long carnival coaster in which individual cars are vertically lifted through a tube and then spiral to the bottom. Brought here in 1992 from Enchanted Forest, it was previously located in Dogpatch USA (Arkansas).

Big Chief Karts & Coasters
P.O. Box 5
Wisconsin Dells, Wisconsin 53965
www.dellschamber.com/bigchief.htm

The Laskaris family established an amusement business in 1972 with the opening of a three-wheeler dirt track next to their Big Chief Restaurant. Today, with two locations and over twenty tracks combined, they have the world's largest collection of go-kart tracks.

CYCLOPS (1995)   The first wooden roller coaster in Wisconsin is 80 feet tall with a 70-foot drop at 50 mph. The 1,700 feet of track follows the terrain in a figure-eight formation as designed by Custom Coasters International.

PEGASUS (1996)   Another CCI design, this one is built over and around two go-kart tracks. Featuring 1,300 feet of undulating track, Pegasus has a 65-foot lift with a 50-foot first drop at 35 mph.

ZEUS (1997)   The third woodie in three years, this out-and-back is built partially over cyclops and then runs into the woods by itself. With a 60 mph, 80-foot first drop from a 90-foot lift, this 2,500-foot-long coaster completes the CCI trifecta.

Riverview Park
P.O. Box 300
Highway 12
Wisconsin Dells, Wisconsin 53965
www.riverviewpark.com

Primarily known for the largest collection of "U-Drive-Em" rides in the state, this fun park also has several amusement rides and waterpark attractions on its 35 acres.

GALAXI (1996)   A steel carnival style roller coaster with 1,650 feet of track laid out in a classic figure-eight, the trains consist of two cars, each with four passenger seats.

Pegasus (Big Chief Karts and Coasters).

Zeus (Big Chief Karts and Coasters).

Roller Coasters in Canada

West Edmonton Mall
#2472, 8882-170 Street
Edmonton, Alberta T5T 4M2
Canada
www.westedmontonmall.com

West Edmonton Mall is a huge complex consisting of recreation, entertainment, and retail. The mall was built in three phases, each opening between 1981 and 1985. Phase II included an indoor amusement park originally called Canada Fantasyland, now renamed Galaxyland. This mall has been listed in the *Guinness Book of World Records* as the largest shopping center in the world.

MINDBENDER (1985)   This is the world's largest triple-looping coaster and is completely enclosed. The 4,198-foot-long track has a first drop from a height of 145 feet and the train can reach a top speed of 65 miles per hour. Designed by Anton Schwarzkopf.

AUTOSLED (1985)   This smooth spiraling steel coaster is 1,170 feet long and was manufactured by Zierer to be a family attraction.

DRAGON WAGON (1992)   A small steel coaster specifically for children.

Playland
P.O. Box 69020
Hastings Park
Vancouver, British Columbia V5K 4W3
Canada
www.pne.bc.ca

An amusement park first known as "Skid Road" opened as part of the first Pacific National Exhibition in 1910. The park was renamed "Happy Land" in 1926 and remained on the original site until 1958 when it was moved to its present site and reopened under the name Playland.

Mindbender (West Edmonton Mall).

COASTER (1958)   This is a classic twisting wooden roller coaster with a 68-foot-tall lift. The old padded trains travel at speeds up to 47 miles per hour over the 2,840-foot-long track.

WILD MOUSE (1958)   The popular "Mad Mouse" coaster has made a recent comeback. This is one of the original designs with the traditional hairpin turns.

CORKSCREW (1984)   A 2,400-foot-long, double corkscrew designed by Vekoma. Relocated here in 1994, from Boblo Island in Detroit, this steel coaster has a height of 75 feet and a top speed of 40 mph.

Coaster (Playland).

Top: Coaster. Bottom: Corkscrew (Playland).

Upper Clements Park

P.O. Box 99
Clementsport, Nova Scotia B0S 1E0
Canada
www.upperclementspark.com

This Nova Scotia park includes the last coaster completely designed by the late William Cobb.

TREE TOPPER (1989)   Cobb's wooden out-and-back uses the hilly terrain to its advantage as it weaves around the trees for 1 minute, 15 seconds. The entire track is 1,400 feet long, has a lift of 60 feet, and reaches a top speed of 35 miles per hour.

Tree Topper (Upper Clements Park).

Marineland
7657 Portage Road
Niagara Falls, Ontario L2E 6X8
Canada

In 1961, John Holer opened this attraction with two water tanks and three sea lions. Today his park combines marine life shows, animal petting areas and a handful of rides including the unusual Dragon Mountain.

DRAGON MOUNTAIN (1983)   Designed by John Holer in conjunction with Arrow/Huss, this multi-inversion steel coaster begins with a 186-foot lift that drops the train 50 miles per hour into a descending double loop. The 5,500 feet of track cover 30 acres and include 1,163 feet of tunnels. The climax of this 3 minute ride is a unique bow-tie loop.

TIVOLI ROLLER COASTER   A 653-foot-long steel coaster specially designed by Zierer for families.

Dragon Mountain (Marineland).

Paramount Canada's Wonderland

P.O. Box 624
958 Jane Street
Vaughan, Ontario LGA 1S6
Canada
www.canadaswonderland.com

Located just outside Toronto, this theme park opened in 1981 and is still Canada's largest with over 300 acres.

DRAGON FYRE (1981)   This 2,160-foot-long steel coaster was designed by Arrow Dynamics and contains a double loop and a corkscrew. The 78-foot-tall lift hill allows the train a top speed of 50 mph.

MIGHTY CANADIAN MINEBUSTER (1981)   Designed by Curtis D. Summers, this large wooden out-and-back is 3,828 feet long, 90 feet tall and has a first drop speed of 62 mph. Plan to spend two minutes, forty seconds on this, the longest roller coaster in the park.

WILDE BEAST (1981)   A 3,150-foot-long wooden double out-and-back with an 82-foot lift hill and a top speed of 56 mph. Designed by Curtis D. Summers and the Philadelphia Toboggan Company, this coaster has a ride time of 2 minutes, 30 seconds.

SKYRIDER (1985)   This is a tubular steel track coaster 2,210 feet long on which riders are secured in a standing position. Designed by Togo, it features one 360-degree vertical loop that follows a 51 mph drop from the 88-foot-tall lift.

THE BAT (1991)   Designed by Vekoma, this coaster turns riders upside down six times in less than 1 minute. It has a boomerang with one vertical loop. It is 875 feet long and has two towers of 125 feet in height.

VORTEX (1991)   This is a suspended steel coaster designed by Arrow. While swinging from side to side as it floats over the ground, the train can reach speeds of 55 mph along the 2,361-foot track.

GHOSTER COASTER (1981)   Philadelphia Toboggan Company's 1,356-foot-long wooden coaster designed for children. The highest point is 41 feet and the top speed is 35 mph.

THUNDER RUN (1986)   A Mack steel family coaster 33 feet tall and 1,083 feet long, this runaway mine train runs one minute, forty-five seconds.

TOP GUN (1995)   Vekoma designed this 2,172-foot-long inverted coaster with five elements that flip you head over heels. From a 102-foot lift hill the suspended chairs drop at 56 mph and begin a 1 minute, 45 second ride.

TAXI JAM (1998)   Designed for parents and children to ride together, this Miler coaster is 205 feet long and runs for only 55 seconds.

Mighty Canadian Minebuster (Paramount Canada's Wonderland).

Top: Wilde Beast. Bottom: Vortex (Paramount Canada's Wonderland).

THE FLY (1999)   This steel coaster follows 1,338 feet of track through hairpin turns, quick twists and a 50-foot drop. The three minute ride was manufactured by Heinrich Mack GMBH & Company.

Top: Top Gun. Bottom: The Fly (Paramount Canada's Wonderland).

La Ronde
Ile Notre-Dame
Montreal, Quebec H3C 1A9
Canada
www.pdi-montreal.com

This is a traditional amusement park that is located on an island. It opened in 1968 on the site of the 1967 World's Fair and today features rides, shows and a water park.

LES PETITES MONTAGNES RUSSES (1967)   An Arrow (Huss) steel coaster designed for children. The 15 mph ride is 426 feet long, 12 feet high and runs for 1 minute, 52 seconds.

LE SUPER MANEGE (1981)   A basic corkscrew design by Vekoma, this two minute ride has a 75-foot lift, 2,400 feet of track, a top speed of 40 mph and duration of 1 minute, 54 seconds.

LE BOOMERANG (1984)   Designed by Vekoma, this steel coaster turns riders upside down six times in less than 1 minute. Riders are first pulled backward up to the top of a nearly vertical eleven-story tower. The train is then released and attains 50 miles per hour, goes through a boomerang and a vertical loop, then heads up another nearly vertical eleven-story tower where the trip begins again — backward!

LE MONSTRE (1985)   Designed by William Cobb, this huge wooden twister has two tracks: the original is 3,965 feet long and the second (added in 1986) is 3,994 feet. From a 132-foot height, these trains drop at 60 mph and weave in and out through the twisting layout, crossing eighteen times during a 2 minute, 45 second run.

LE DRAGON (1994)   This smooth steel Intamin coaster is 1,100 feet long, 50 feet high, has a top speed of 30 mph, and the entire 2 minute ride is housed indoors.

LE COBRA (1987)   Relocated here in 1995, this single-looping "stand-up" coaster covers 2,575 feet of track during two minutes. Literally standing, you accelerate down from 87 feet at 48 mph into the 72-foot-high loop. Intamin designed this roller coaster for those who can stand it!

Le Boomerang (Bernard Brault).

Le Monstre (Bernard Brault).

Le Cobra (Johanne Palasse).

Appendix 1
Famous Roller Coaster Designers

The annals of roller coaster lore are highlighted by famous designers who tried their hands at creating coasters that could deliver the most thrills and chills.

Philadelphia Toboggan Company has long been one of the leading coaster designers. The firm, working with designers such as Herbert Schmeck and John Allen, crafted such coasters as the Wildcat (1927) at Lake Compounce Festival Park in Bristol, Connecticut, a classic example of the Golden Age of coaster architecture. The company also created the Giant (1917) at Paragon Park (moved to Wild World in Mitchellville, Maryland, and renamed Wild One); Flying Comet (1940) at Whalom Park in Fitchburg, Massachusetts; the Great American Scream Machine (1973) at Six Flags Over Georgia in Atlanta; and numerous others.

Frank Prior and Frederick Church were a renowned coaster design team that created many classic coasters. Giant Dipper (1925) at Belmont Park in San Diego, California, was one of their masterpieces.

Arthur Looff was one of the Golden Age coaster designers, famous for building the Giant Dipper at Santa Cruz Beach Boardwalk in Santa Cruz, California. Looff envisioned a giant wooden roller coaster that would be a "combination of earthquake, balloon ascension, and aeroplane drop." In 1987, the Giant Dipper was honored as a National Historic Landmark.

E. Joy Morris designed Leap-the-Dips (1902) at Lakemont Park in Altoona, Pennsylvania, the world's oldest coaster still operating and the only remaining "side friction figure-eight," which was a popular design style from about 1900 to 1920.

Ed Vettel designed the famous Blue Streak (1937) at Conneaut Lake Park, Pennsylvania, which is noted for its unique "camel humps"—a series of three dramatic hills that occur in breathtakingly quick succession on the "out" side of the ride's 2,900-foot-long circuit. Ed Vettel's nephew, Andy Vettel, has continued the family tradition, designing coasters such as Thunderbolt (1968) at Kennywood in West Mifflin, Pennsylvania.

Miller and Baker was one of America's top coaster firms, creating such coasters as Jack Rabbit (1922) at Kennywood in West Mifflin, Pennsylvania, which was designed by John A. Miller.

Arrow Dynamics was at the forefront of the revival in roller coaster popularity. Arrow has created many of the quintessential coaster designs currently thrilling riders from Disneyland to Dollywood. Arrow conceived the runaway mine train–style of coaster, such as Cedar Creek Mine Ride (1969) at Cedar Point in Sandusky, Ohio. Arrow also designed the magnificent $8 million Magnum XL-200 (1989) at Cedar Point, which was listed in the 1990 *Guinness Book of World Records* as the world's fastest coaster with the longest drop.

Bolliger & Mabillard of Switzerland have designed numerous coasters, including Batman: The Ride (1992) at Six Flags Great America in Gurnee, Illinois, the world's first inverted outside looping roller coaster. Recently the firm has introduced the floorless coaster with Medusa (1999) at Six Flags Great Adventure in New Jersey and Kraken (2000) at SeaWorld in Florida.

Anton Schwarzkopf of Germany designed many U.S. theme park coasters. His Revolution (1976) at Six Flags Magic Mountain in Valencia, California, was the world's first giant looping roller coaster with G-forces of 4.94 when entering the loop.

Curtis D. Summers designed Mean Streak (1991) at Cedar Point in Sandusky, Ohio, one of the world's tallest wooden coasters. Mean Streak was constructed by the Charles Dinn Corporation.

National Amusement Device Company created many coasters for American theme parks, the last being the woodie Wildcat (1968) now at Frontier City in Oklahoma City, Oklahoma.

Custom Coasters International built their first in 1992, the Sky Princess at Dutch Wonderland in Lancaster, Pennsylvania. Founded by Denise Dinn Larrick, the daughter of Charles Dinn, CCI has gone on to create many more wooden roller coasters.

International Coaster, Inc., created, among other coasters, the Hurler (1994), a massive 3,157-foot-long woodie at Paramount's Carowinds and Kings Dominion.

O.D. Hopkins Associates, created the Texas Tornado (1985) at Wonderland Park in Amarillo, Texas, which includes a 200-foot long tunnel 13 feet under the ground.

John Pierce & Associates designed Rattler (1992) at Fiesta Texas in San Antonio, Texas. Built by the Roller Coaster Corporation of Texas, this mammoth coaster is built around a limestone quarry and includes tunnels within the quarry walls. It opened with four world records: the tallest wooden coaster; longest first drop of any woodie; fastest woodie; and the steepest first drop of a wooden coaster.

William Cobb created numerous coasters, the last of which was the Tree Topper (1989) at Upper Clements Park in Clementsport, Nova Scotia, Canada.

Vekoma International of the Netherlands was established in 1926 as a manufacturer of agricultural equipment but eventually shifted to the amusement industry. Designer of numerous coasters, they are perhaps best known for the boomerang, located at parks worldwide.

D.H. Morgan Manufacturing builds several types of amusement rides including the hypercoaster. With a 207-foot-tall lift, Wild Thing (1996) at Valleyfair is a good example.

Premier Rides has literally launched onto the scene with the introduction of Linear Induction Motors. Mr. Freeze (1998) at Six Flags St. Louis propels riders from zero to 70 miles per hour within four seconds.

Great Coasters International has put the twist in several modern wooden twisters such as Wildcat (1996) at Hersheypark, Pennsylvania, and Roar (1998) at Six Flags America in Maryland.

Appendix 2

The Longest Roller Coasters in North America

These fifteen roller coasters are the longest in terms of length of track.

Coaster	*Material*	*Length*
Beast	Wood	7400
Son of Beast	Wood	7032
Millennium Force	Steel	6595
Desperado	Steel	5900
Mamba	Steel	5600
Steel Force	Steel	5600
Dragon Mountain	Steel	5500
Wild Thing	Steel	5460
Mean Streak	Wood	5427
Shivering Timbers	Wood	5384
Superman-Ride of Steel	Steel	5350
Magnum XL-200	Steel	5105
Rattler	Wood	5080
Raging Bull	Steel	5057
Texas Giant	Wood	4920

Appendix 3

Numbers of Coasters per State and Province

State/Province	Wood	Steel	Total
Alabama	2	1	3
Alberta	0	4	4
Arizona	0	2	2
Arkansas	1	0	1
British Columbia	1	3	4
California	44	7	51
Colorado	2	8	10
Connecticut	2	2	4
Delaware	0	1	1
Florida	2	14	16
Georgia	3	13	16
Idaho	2	3	5
Illinois	4	10	14
Indiana	3	5	8
Iowa	4	4	8
Kansas	1	1	2
Kentucky	2	4	6
Louisiana	1	6	7
Maine	1	3	4
Maryland	2	10	12
Massachusetts	3	6	9
Michigan	3	3	6
Minnesota	1	6	7
Mississippi	0	1	1
Missouri	2	9	11
Nevada	0	7	7
New Brunswick	0	1	1
New Hampshire	1	5	6
New Jersey	3	28	31
New Mexico	0	1	1
New York	7	23	30
North Carolina	3	5	8

State/Province	Wood	Steel	Total
Nova Scotia	1	0	1
Ohio	12	26	38
Oklahoma	2	4	6
Ontario	3	17	20
Oregon	0	3	3
Pennsylvania	17	22	39
Prince Edward Island	0	1	1
Quebec	1	6	7
Rhode Island	0	1	1
South Carolina	2	6	8
Tennessee	2	3	5
Texas	4	34	38
Utah	1	5	6
Virginia	4	11	15
Washington	1	5	6
West Virginia	2	1	3
Wisconsin	3	4	7
Total	118	387	505

Appendix 4

Chronology of Wooden Coasters Still in Operation

Built	Roller Coaster
1902	Leap-the-Dips, Lakemont Park, Altoona, PA
1915	Zippin Pippin, Libertyland, Memphis, TN
1917	Wild One, Six Flags America, Largo, MD (re-opened 1986)
1919	Jack Rabbit, Clementon Lake, Clementon, NJ
1920	Jack Rabbit, Seabreeze, Rochester, NY
1921	Jack Rabbit, Kennywood, West Mifflin, PA
1921	The Roller Coaster, Lagoon, Farmington, UT
1923	Thunderhawk, Dorney Park, Allentown, PA
1924	Thunderbolt, Kennywood, West Mifflin, PA
1924	Giant Dipper, Santa Cruz Beach Boardwalk, Santa Cruz, CA
1925	Giant Dipper, Belmont Park, San Diego, CA
1926	The Big Dipper, Geauga Lake, Aurora, OH
1927	Screechin' Eagle, Americana, Middletown, OH
1927	Giant Coaster, Arnold's Park, Arnold's Park, IA
1927	Cyclone, Astroland, Coney Island, NY
1927	The Racer, Kennywood, West Mifflin, PA
1927	The Wildcat, Lake Compounce Festival Park, Bristol, CT
1928	Kiddie Coaster, Playland Park, Rye, NY
1929	Dragon Coaster, Playland Park, Rye, NY
1929	Cyclone, Williams Grove, Williams Grove, PA
1930	The Yankee Cannonball, Canobie Lake Park, Salem, NH
1935	Roller Coaster, The Puyallup Fair, Puyallup, WA
1937	Blue Streak, Conneaut Lake Park, Conneaut Lake Park, PA
1938	Rollo Coaster, Idlewild, Ligonier, PA
1940	Flyer Comet, Whalom Park, Fitchburg, MA
1940	Cyclone Coaster, Lakeside, Denver, CO
1941	Thunderbolt, Riverside, Agawam, MA
1947	Comet, The Great Escape, Lake George, NY (from Crystal Beach)
1947	Phoenix, Knoebel's Amusement Resort, Elysburg, PA (reopened in 1985)

Built	Roller Coaster
1949	Roller Coaster, Joyland, Wichita, KS
1949	Coaster, Playland, Vancouver, BC
1950	Little Dipper, Kiddieland, Melrose, IL
1951	Comet, Waldameer Park, Erie, PA
1952	Little Dipper, Hillcrest Park, Lemont, IL
1956	Sea Dragon, Wyandot Lake, Powel, OH
1958	Big Dipper, Camden Park, Huntington, WV
1960	Skyliner, Lakemont Park, Altoona, PA
1961	Lil' Dipper, Camden Park, Huntington, WV
1963	Starliner, Miracle Strip, Panama City, FL
1964	The Blue Streak, Cedar Point, Sandusky, OH
1966	Swamp Fox, Family Kingdom, Myrtle Beach, SC
1967	Cannonball, Lake Winnepesaukah, Rossville, GA
1968	Wildcat, Frontier City, Oklahoma City, OK
1968	Zingo, Bell's Amusement Park, Tulsa, OK
1972	The Beastie, Paramount's Kings Island, Kings Island, OH
1972	The Racer, Paramount's Kings Island, Kings Island, OH
1973	The Great American Scream Machine, Six Flags Over Georgia, Atlanta, GA
1974	Scooby Doo, Paramount's Kings Dominion, Doswell, VA
1974	Rebel Yell, Paramount's Kings Dominion, Doswell, VA
1975	High Roller, Valleyfair, Shakopee, MN
1975	Scooby Doo's Ghoster Coaster, Paramount's Carowinds, Charlotte, NC
1976	Screamin' Eagle, Six Flags Over Mid America, Eureka, MO
1976	Texas Cyclone, Astroworld, Houston, TX
1976	Thunder Road, Paramount's Carowinds, Charlotte, NC
1978	Arkansas Twister, Magic Springs, Hot Springs, AR (from Boardwalk and Baseball in Florida, "Hurricane")
1978	Colossus, Six Flags Magic Mountain, Valencia, CA
1978	Tornado, Adventureland, Des Moines, IA
1979	The Beast, Paramount's Kings Island, Kings Island, OH
1979	Rolling Thunder, Six Flags Great Adventure, Jackson, NJ
1980	Judge Roy Scream, Six Flags Over Texas, Arlington, TX
1981	Ghoster Coaster, Paramount's Canada's Wonderland, Vaughan, ONT
1981	Mighty Canadian Minebuster, Paramount's Canada's Wonderland, Vaughan, ONT
1981	Wilde Beast, Paramount's Canada's Wonderland, Vaughan, ONT
1981	American Eagle, Six Flags Great America, Gurnee, IL
1982	The Grizzly, Paramount's Kings Dominion, Doswell, VA
1983	The Riverside Cyclone, Riverside Amusement Park, Agawam, MA
1985	Le Monstre, La Ronde, Montreal, QUE
1986	The Grizzly, Paramount's Great America, Santa Clara, CA
1988	The Raging Wolf Bobs, Gauge Lake, Aurora, OH
1988	Wolverine Wildcat, Michigan's Adventure, Muskegon, MI
1989	Timber Wolf, Worlds of Fun, Kansas City, MO
1989	Hercules, Dorney Park, Allentown, PA

Built	*Roller Coaster*
1989	Tree Topper, Upper Clements Theme Park, Clementsport, NS
1990	Predator, Darien Lake, Darien Center, NY
1990	Georgia Cyclone, Six Flags Over Georgia, Atlanta, GA
1990	Thunder Run, Kentucky Kingdom, Louisville, KY
1990	Texas Giant, Six Flags Over Texas, Arlington, TX
1991	Psyclone, Six Flags Magic Mountain, Valencia, CA
1991	The Mean Streak, Cedar Point, Sandusky, OH
1992	Sky Princess, Dutch Wonderland, Lancaster, PA
1992	Rattler, Fiesta Texas, San Antonio, TX
1993	The Outlaw, Adventureland, Des Moines, IA
1994	The Hoosier Hurricane, Indiana Beach, Monticello, IN
1994	The Hurler, Paramount's Kings Dominion, Doswell, VA
1994	The Hurler, Paramount's Carowinds, Charlotte, NC
1994	Zach's Zoomer, Michigan's Adventure, Muskegon, MI
1995	Twister II, Six Flags Elitch Gardens, Denver, CO
1995	Cyclops, Big Chief Karts & Coasters, Wisconsin Dells, WI
1995	Cannonball Run, Waterville USA, Gulf Shores, AL
1995	Viper, Six Flags Great America, Gurnee, IL
1995	Raven, Holiday World, Santa Claus, IN
1996	Underground, Adventureland, Des Moines, IA
1996	Timber Terror, Silverwood Theme Park, Athol, ID
1996	Pegasus, Big Chief Karts & Coasters, Wisconsin Dells, WI
1996	Great White, Morey's Pier, Wildwood, NJ
1996	Wildcat, Hersheypark, Hershey, PA
1997	Zeus, Big Chief Karts & Coasters, Wisconsin Dells, WI
1998	Shivering Timbers, Michigan's Adventure, Muskegon, MI
1998	Roar, Six Flags America, Largo, MD
1998	Rampage, VisionLand, Bessemer, AL
1998	Excalibur, Funtown/Splashtown USA, Saco, ME
1998	Twisted Sisters, Six Flags Kentucky Kingdom, Louisville, KY
1998	Ghost Rider, Knott's Berry Farm, Buena Park, CA
1999	Silver Comet, Martin's Fantasy Island, Grand Island, NY
1999	Roar, Six Flags Marine World, Vallejo, CA
1999	Tremors, Silverwood Theme Park, Athol, ID
1999	Gwazi, Busch Gardens Tampa, Tampa, FL
1999	Twister, Knoebel's Amusement Resort, Elysburg, PA
2000	Son of Beast, Paramount's Kings Island, Kings Island, OH
2000	The Intimidator, Winston Cup Race World, Pigeon Forge, TN
2000	Boulder Dash, Lake Compounce, Bristol, CT
2000	The Legend, Holiday World, Santa Claus, IN
2000	Mega Zeph, Jazzland Theme Park, New Orleans, LA
2000	Lightning Racer, Hersheypark, Hershey, PA
2000	Hurricane Category 5, Myrtle Beach Pavilion, Myrtle Beach, SC

Appendix 5

Interesting Roller Coaster Facts

• The "father of gravity," La Marcus Adna Thompson, was only 36 years old when he built his first roller coaster in 1884.

• The history of Arrow Dynamics includes a 1978 move to Utah and two name changes. Before becoming Arrow Dynamics, a merger in 1981 converted Arrow Development into Arrow/Huss.

• The Paul L. Ruben Archives has in its collection over 16,000 roller coaster images worldwide.

• Arrow Dynamics' first suspended roller coaster previewed at Kings Island in 1981. Appropriately named The Bat, this prototype only ran until the end of the 1983 season.

• What's in a name? In 1931 the community known as Kilbourn, Wisconsin, changed its name to what is now referred to as the Wisconsin Dells.

• In 1998, Premier Parks, Inc., finalized their acquisition of Six Flags Theme Parks. This $1.9 billion deal was the largest in the history of the amusement industry.

• Just to make it official the Cyclone at Coney Island was designated a National Historic Landmark on June 26, 1991.

• What's in a name? Michigan's Adventure retained Custom Coasters International to build Zack's Zoomer, named after the park owner's son.

• United States patent #3,114,332 describing a "bobsled amusement ride" was issued to Karl Bacon and Edgor Morgan of Arrow Development (Dynamics) in 1963.

• And the award for the best roller coaster in a 3-D movie goes to— Atom Smasher! *This Is Cinerama* opened in 1952 featuring this ride from Rockaway's Playland in Queens, N.Y.

• The original corkscrew roller coaster designed by Arrow Dynamics was located at Knott's Berry Farm from 1975 to 1989. Today it operates in Idaho at Silverwood Theme Park.

• Established in 1846, the oldest continually operating amusement park in North America is Lake Compounce in Bristol, Connecticut.

• The National Amusement Device Company was founded by Aurel Vaszin in 1925. Originally this Ohio firm was named the Dayton Fun House and Riding Device Manufacturing Company.

• The American Coaster Enthusiast (ACE) is a club formed in 1978 at Busch

Gardens in Williamsburg, Virginia. For membership information contact:

American Coaster Enthusiasts
P.O. Box 8226
Chicago, Illinois 60680

• The first patent granted for a roller coaster in the United States was in 1872. Described as an incline railway, patent #128,674 was issued to J.G. Taylor.

• There were twelve Flip Flap coasters created in Toledo, Ohio, during the 1890s. The most notable was the one located at Sea Lion Park in 1895.

• Two different coasters with the same name. Before the high-tech "Rock 'N' Roller Coaster" at the Disney-MGM Studios opened, there was the low-tech "Rock 'N' Roller Coaster" (1972–1998) at the defunct Opryland USA.

• As a symbolic gesture to recapture the magic of the original Mr. Twister, a single bolt was removed from this classic coaster before demolition and installed in Knoebels' new Twister.

• Although The Beast holds the record for wooden coasters at 7,400 feet, the world's longest is a steel roller coaster. The Ultimate at Lightwater Valley Theme Park in North Yorkshire, England, is 7,498 feet long.

• When testing the Hoosier Hurricane, CCI used bags of corn instead of the traditional sand bags. Corn doesn't get into the wheel bearings like sand can and any spillage is taken care of by birds.

• The trains on the Screechin' Eagle at Americana Amusement Park in Middletown, Ohio, are from the Wildcat (1926–1994) at the original Elitch Gardens site in Denver, Colorado.

• A city ordinance in Tulsa, Oklahoma, specifically limits the hours of operation for the roller coaster at Bell's Amusement Park. Resulting from a neighborhood lawsuit and subsequent ruling, Zingo has a 9:00 P.M. curfew lifted only during fair week.

• By 1972, when The Racer opened at Kings Island, the number of wooden roller coasters had dwindled to fewer than 100 from a previous high of almost 2,000.

• Who has had a roller coaster named in their honor?

A. Vincent Price (The Screamer)

B. Elvis Presley (Rock 'N' Roller)

C. Dale Earnhardt (The Intimidator)

D. Judy Garland (Twister)

The answer is somewhere among these pages!

• Waterpark equipment manufacturer NBGS International designed the Master Blaster, the world's first water coaster, in 1994. Evolving from the water slide, this pattern sounds similar to roller coaster development. What's next … inverted water slides?

• Thunder Road, the wooden twin-track racing out-and-back at Paramounts Carowinds, was themed after the Robert Mitchum movie of the same name.

Index